The Gap

A Scholarly Work on Executive Women

Dr. Wendy James, Ph.D.

Other Books by Dr. Wendy James, Ph.D.

The Princess Chronicles
A Bedside Companion

ABSTRACT

This qualitative study investigated the experiences of executive women and their choices in balancing work with marriage and children. Research on women in the workplace tends to conflate categories of hourly workers, part-time employees, and middle- and upper-management careers. Yet, the literature on balancing career and family life does not adequately portray the experiences of executive women. The purpose of the study was to discover executive women's perceptions about their career, how they chose their path, and how their career choices affected their decisions about marriage and children. The research questions for this study examined: (a) The effect of executive women's career choices on their balance of marriage and children, (b) reflection on career choices as an opportunity (enhancement) or loss (conflict) regarding marriage and children, and (c) the sacrifices made or regrets felt, if any, by executive women in pursuing a career. The research questions reflect the study's grounding in role theory, role conflict theory, and spillover theory. Data were collected via personal interviews with participants, which were recorded, transcribed, and coded for themes. Results showed that although participants were conscious of making some sacrifices, such as feeling guilt missing their children's events and not making time for self or women friends and feeling some guilt about those sacrifices, they expressed no regrets for the decisions they made. The study has the potential to effect social change by providing insight about how an important subset of the professional work force attempts to balance career and family life. The study may also help women pursuing business careers make more informed choices about their personal and professional goals.

TABLE OF CONTENTS

LIST OF FIGURES

CHAPTER 1: INTRODUCTION TO THE STUDY

Introduction

Executive women have focused on their careers, yet at what cost to their personal relationships? The goal of this dissertation was to examine the choices executive women make in their careers and how those choices affect decisions regarding marriage and children. For the purpose of this study, executive women were defined as women over 35 years old who have held supervisory positions in business for at least 10 years. These include CEOs, presidents, vice presidents, managers, and supervisors. These women were not involved in the professions (e.g., those careers that rely on individual billing for services performed, such as attorneys, physicians, psychologists, real estate agents, CPAs, among others). Professionals who bill hourly might work part-time to pursue family interests. Consequently, many women may choose professions that allow them to balance marriage and children. However conversely, executive women have chosen a career path requiring extensive hours and travel and may have chosen to balance family with career. Based on this assumption, the literature makes no distinction between those women who work because they have to help support their family and those in leadership roles who work for the intrinsic rewards of having a career and who have devoted at least 10 years to their career. Because the latter is a relatively new group, there is a gap in the literature pertaining to executive women (Hewlett & Luce, 2006; Hochschild, 1997; Kiecolt, 2003).

Feminist theory has emphasized creating equal opportunities for women in education and the work place, including the corporate world. The influence of feminism has led to studies on gender and management (Berdahl & Anderson, 2005; Hyde, 2005), success at work (Goren, 2003; Kirchmeyer, 2002; Ragins & Cotton, 1999), and enhancement and self-esteem in the work force (Jackson & Scharman, 2002; Jones, Braithwaite, & Healy, 2003; Kiecolt, 2003; Tiedje et al., 1990). Dual-earner families make up 68% of married couples with children under age 18 (Perrone, Civiletto, Webb, & Fitch, 2004). Women's increasing presence in the work force has led to concerns with work-family balance (Caprara, Regalia, Scabini, Barbarnelli, & Bandura, 2004; Spitze, 1988; Warner, Winter, & Breshears, 2005). Women have moved into influential and leadership roles expanding the general concepts of feminist theory.

Much work-family research has been based on three theories: role theory, role conflict theory, and spillover theory. These theories focus on conflict (loss) and enhancement (opportunity) in maintaining career and family balance. Most work-family research has combined divorced and single mothers and fathers, part-time and full-time workers, and employees at all levels, from hourly wage-earners to managers (Caprara et al., 2004; Spitze, 1988; Warner et al., 2005). Executive women are an emerging group, and it has taken a generation to see the fruits of their labors. The decisions these women have made about work and family are neither right nor wrong in terms of some overarching cultural norm. Instead, shifting norms mean that individual choices must be evaluated as society gives more opportunities for women to make choices about their future (Hewlett; 2002; Higgins, Duxbury, & Lee, 2001). This study sought to determine how executive women have made choices about their careers and the effect their decisions have had on marriage and family life

Problem Statement

Historically in the United States, women have fulfilled the traditional roles of wife and mother, and evolutionary theory explained this behavior. When women entered the work force and gained the education and experience to compete in the marketplace, feminist theory explained that behavior. As more dual-income families appeared, role theory and spillover theory explained that phenomenon. The emergence of executive women prompts a reexamination of the theories used to explain workforce behavior. It has taken a generation for these women to reach executive levels. They are in a position to reflect on the role work has played in their lives. Until recently it was an anomaly for women to be in supervisory positions; women had not spent the business years necessary to move from entry level positions to reach high-end executive positions. As a result, there is a gap in the literature regarding executive women and the choices they have made. How has their work affected their choices to marry and have children? While research on working women exists, it does not typically include executive women.

Much remains to be learned about the tradeoffs executive women make, their attitudes toward a historically patriarchal marketplace, the extent to which they see career and family as antagonistic or complementary endeavors, and how well they were able to anticipate the challenges they would face as executives. In light of this disparity, how do women executives balance career, marriage, and family? To answer these questions, the researcher interviewed executive women using the phenomenological approach.

Nature of the Study

This qualitative, phenomenological study analyzed a group of executive women to discover their rationales for career and family decisions. The phenomenological approach attempted to offer insight into the essence of executive women. The study used the tenets of role theory, role conflict theory, and spillover theory to determine if the conflict (losses) and enhancement (opportunities) specified in the literature were prevalent for this group. New themes and concepts evolved during the study.

Executive women ages 35-60 were interviewed about their status in the business world and how it has affected their ability to balance career, marriage, and children. Interviews reflected the transcendental, phenomenological method, with open-ended questions that prompted participants to explain their experience in achieving their career accomplishments. Interview questions were designed to enable participants to discuss the trials and tribulations of their careers and how they arrived at their current position. The goal was to further understand the decision making process as they moved up in their business as it relates to decisions on relationships, marriage, and children.

Research Questions

1. How have executive women made choices about careers, and how have those decisions affected the way they balance marriage and children?

2. How have career choices been an opportunity (enhancement) or loss (conflict) regarding marriage and children?

3. What sacrifices have executive women made in pursuing a career, and what regrets do they have, if any?

Purpose of the Study

The purpose of this qualitative, phenomenological study was to explore the choices executive women have made in balancing career with marriage and children. The study attempted to increase understanding of how choices at work have affected participants' attempts to balance career with family life. The study focused on the constructs of conflict (loss) and enhancement (opportunities) women experience, and analyzed participants' responses in light of role theory, role conflict theory, and spillover theory.

By relating their experiences, participants were able to describe the choices they made as executives, wives, and mothers. These women, age 35 to 60, are among the first group to have spent significant time in business management roles and to have been confronted with decisions on marriage and children. The focus on executive women was twofold: (a) to ascertain their perspective on how career affects choices regarding marriage and children, and (b) to determine if secondary issues (e.g., losses, opportunities, sacrifices, and regrets) affected the balance of career and family life.

Definition of Terms

The following terms were provisionally defined and then clarified by the researcher as interview results were analyzed.

Balance: The ability to handle multiple roles, for example, executive, wife, and mother. The focus of this study was on whether an executive woman perceives that she has balanced career and family (Tiedje et al., 1990).

Career woman: Any woman working part- or full-time in the work force at some point in her life (Goren, 2003; Kirchmeyer, 2002; Ragins & Cotton, 1999).

Executive women: Women over 35 years old who have held supervisory positions, have achieved significant influence and financial success, and have been in their industry in a supervisory position for at least 10 years. Executive women have typically carved a path into upper management that requires extensive hours and offers little flexibility from their employers. These women are not involved in the professions ((e.g., those careers that rely on individual billing for services performed, such as attorneys, physicians, psychologists, real estate agents, CPAs, among others). Executive women have extended work hours and travel that distinguish them from women in professional services. They include CEOs, presidents, vice presidents, managers, and supervisors (Hewlett & Luce, 2005; Lyness & Judiesch, 2001).

Happiness: A sense of accomplishment and satisfaction in one's achievements. "Those who experience a preponderance of positive emotions tend to be successful and accomplished across multiple life domains" (Lyubomirsky, King, & Diener, 2005, p. 803).

Life satisfaction: A satisfying role with positive spillover. Potential roles are executive, mother, and wife. Satisfaction may be considered separately for career and home life. For example, work and home (dis)satisfaction are two separate considerations, although there is often spillover between the two, which affects satisfaction in general (Heller & Watson, 2005; Kiecolt, 2003). Although some research distinguishes between happiness and life satisfaction, in this study the two were coded as one construct.

Limitations and Assumptions

The study used criterion sampling and convenience sampling. Criterion sampling was applied because all executive women included in this study had worked in corporate environments in supervisory positions for at least 10 years, which means they had all experienced the same phenomenon (Creswell, 2007). The use of convenience sampling and a small sample size, however, may limit the extent to which results can be generalized to other women beyond executive women.

The definition of *executive woman* was developed knowledge acquired from the literature review. The researcher's experience working with women in various business contacts could have biased her definition. Furthermore, the sample was a convenience sample selected by personal contact information known to the researcher by virtue of working with business leaders in major industries. Executive women represented a gap in the literature and were relevant to the nature of phenomenology. The researcher has an etic view that was part of the emic view of the phenomenon. The etic view is the researcher's experience with the phenomenon, and the emic view is the natural setting that allows participants to provide their lived experiences of the phenomenon. It was necessary for the researcher to have knowledge of the target population to distinguish relevant and irrelevant facts in order to extract meaning from the data (Strauss & Corbin, 1990). The researcher attempted to operate in light of an intention expressed by Moustakas (1994):

> I must first explicate my own intentional consciousness through the transcendental processes before I can understand someone or something that is not my own. . . . My own perception is primary; it includes the perception of the other by analogy. (p. 37)

The researcher interviewed executive women with acknowledgement that her perception may be different from the experiences other women revealed in the business world.

The researchers' assumption was women who attained corporate leadership positions were so busy they would delay having children. She assumed the concentration on career would overshadow the ability to have success in both marriage, and child rearing. She assumed that career women would delay having children until they were in their 30s and 40s when they would contemplate the importance of family. The researcher based her experience as the only female in a male dominated Fortune 100 broadcast company. Her contact with female executives revealed they were single or married and without children. Their focus and concentration were on career. The purpose was to take a sampling of executive women who held supervisory positions in a variety of corporate industries and who were married with children to find out how they were able to move up the ladder and "have it all". To maintain impartiality, the researcher targeted none of the interviewees for their sexual orientation or race.

Participants were selected in a convenience sample that depended on contacts in the corporate world and their recommendations of women who met the study's criteria. By virtue of their achievements and promotions within a corporate organization, the interviewees fell within the parameters outlined in the researcher's IRB application. That none of the interviewees were homosexual or outside the European-American descent may not be the fault of the sample but the fault of corporate America to provide diversity in the ranks of women in their promotion or lack thereof of the same. Each generation should progress and benefit from past generations and changes in limitations on hiring and promotions. Further research to focus on specifics of executive women would provide additional documentation.

Significance of Study

There is a gap in the literature regarding how executive women's career choices affect marriage and family life. The literature describes career women broadly, including part-time and full-time positions at all occupational levels, even though it is clear that a woman working part-time has more time for family than does one working full-time.

Executive women are a new and growing group. The typical executive woman has responsibilities (extended work hours, work emergencies, travel) that differ from some other career women. This qualitative study sheds new light on this important and growing group. By encouraging women to describe their life journeys, the researcher discovered themes and patterns that illuminate the difficult process of achieving balance between career and family goals. The goal was to discover if executive women see career as an enhancement or an impediment to marriage and children. It is hoped that this study will expand researchers' knowledge of executive women to contribute to existing theories or add new theories to the literature.

This study should be valuable for executive women struggling to balance career and family. It focused on decisions they have made throughout their careers to reach high-level positions, as well as the effects of those choices on their marital and family relationships. Women make up approximately half the population in the United States, yet they represent a small portion of executives (Johnston, 2007). Because executive women wield power that affects not only the organizations in which they work but also other women who have their own struggles to balance career and family, there is a growing need to better understand this group. The purpose of this study was to determine whether executive women in pursuing their career goals express common themes in their decisions about balancing career and family.

Social Change

Executive women over 35 who have struggled to balance career and family represent a valuable but insufficiently understood resource. Experienced executive women, defined as those who have been in the business world for 10 or more years, have gained valuable experience in pursuing their careers. The unique experiences and perspectives of women as opposed to men have generated considerable research interest (Archer, 1996; Buffardi, Smith, O'Brien, & Erdwins, 1999; Kirchmeyer, 2002; Livingston et al., 1996).

The obstacles facing women in the workplace have been well-documented. The feminist movement has evolved from simply documenting the implicit and explicit discrimination women have experienced to encompassing women advocating for social change that will improve their prospects for career fulfillment. But while feminism has sought to empower women by creating a more level playing field, it has also complicated women's lives by increasing the choices they have, both personally and professionally. The feminist movement paved the road to a variety of destinations other than motherhood and homemaking. Role theory, role conflict theory, and spillover theory predict that conflict (loss), opportunity (enhancement), or both will affect the balance of work with family. This study has the potential to enhance social change by providing information that will be useful to executive and career women attempting to achieve balance in all facets of their lives. It would also be relevant to human resources personnel and companies striving to attract and retain motivated and successful female executive employees.

Summary

This study used interviews of a small group of executive women to shed light on patterns and themes in the choices they make in balancing career with marriage and family. The goal was to discover participants' perceptions about their career: how they chose their current path and how their career choices affected decisions about marriage and children. The study explored how career choices were affected by enhancement opportunity) or conflict (loss). Although there is abundant research on career and family, there is a gap in research on executive women.

Chapter 1 described the problem that gave rise to this study, the nature and purpose of the study, the targeted population, and the study's significance and potential to effect social change. Chapter 2 is a review of the relevant literature, divided into three main areas: dual-income families, career and family conflict, and women's career paths. The chapter also describes the study's theoretical underpinnings by examining role theory, role conflict theory, and spillover theory. Chapter 3 describes the study's methods, including data collection and analysis. Chapter 4 summarizes the study's results, and chapter 5 draws conclusions and presents suggestions for additional research.

CHAPTER 2: LITERATURE REVIEW

Introduction

Women's presence in the work force continues to increase, and their difficulty in balancing the roles of employee, spouse, and mother increases as well. Women have moved into the work force in greater numbers, which has resulted in more research on work and family balance. This chapter reviews that research, in particular the experiences of women as they move into management roles, the barriers that women face in the workplace, and the challenges of balancing work and family. The review begins with a consideration of how the feminist movement paved the way for increasing female participation in the labor force. It then analyzes the dynamics of dual-income families and women's attempts to balance work and family life. The literature search included peer-reviewed articles, many of which were obtained through PsycARTICLES and PsycINFO (1983-2008). Professional books and related Internet sources supplemented these articles.

Feminist Movement

The feminist movement in the United States began with a fight for women's right to vote. Later, the Women's Bureau of the Department of Labor was established as an advocate for women at work. During the 1960s, the feminist movement flowered in an overall climate of social change. The Commission on the Status of Women issued a report in 1963 that documented discrimination against women in America. Since then, state and local governments have established their own commissions for women to assist them in pursuing advanced education and careers. The Civil Rights Act of 1964 prevented employment discrimination on the basis of sex, race, religion, and national origin. Education codes developed in the 1970s provided equal educational opportunities for women. By the 1990s, women were prominent in the corporate world and being elected to public office at all levels of government (Eagly, 1995; Jost & Kay, 2005; Snyder, 2003).

In the 1990s the *mommy track* had become a buzzword, while many women attempted to do it all by refusing to sacrifice marriage and family life to the growing demands of the work world. As women entered the professions, trades, and businesses of every kind, organizations arose to help provide equal opportunities for them regarding career-related issues. Five years ago it was estimated that over 3 million women worked in occupations considered nontraditional (Simpson & Stroh, 2004). The feminist movement continues the social change initiative of enhancing women's rights throughout the world.

Dual-Income Women Move into the Work Force

The prevalence of dual-income families is increasing in the work force (Perrone, Civiletto, Webb, & Fitch, 2004). The U.S. Bureau of the Census (2000) concluded that 65% of all married couples in their 30s are dual-earner couples. Dual-earner families make up 68% of married couples with children under age 18 (Perrone et al., 2004). Because traditionally women have participated in the labor force less than men have, the increase in dual-earner couples reflects the fact that women's participation in the labor force is growing at a faster rate than men's participation. Barnett (2004) predicted that by 2008, women would represent 48% of the labor force, a projection that has proved accurate.

Labor force participation is, in part, a function of educational attainment. According to the U.S. Department of Labor, women have achieved parity with men in receiving bachelor's degrees and doctoral degrees in law and medicine (Barnett, 2004,

p. 159). Educational attainment increases career choices.

Much of the traditional literature on work and family balance, as well as role

theory, reflected patriarchal assumptions about Western culture. But the traditional

pattern has changed. The view of women as focused on home and career to supplement

the family income does not characterize executive women. Wentling (1998) noted that

fewer than 10% of U.S. families fit the once-traditional pattern of breadwinner husband

and stay-at-home wife. Women seeking traditional positions as described above, typically

expect that family will precede career, whereas women who seek nontraditional career

positions plan families later in life with fewer children and are more likely to share

household obligations with their husbands (Cinamon, 2006). For many women, who

choose non-traditional careers it means making difficult choices about career, marriage,

and family (Hakim, 2006).

Career and Family Balance

Prior to the 1970s, it was an anomaly for women to obtain advanced degrees and

move up the executive ladder. By the 1990s, statistics indicated that most women would

have to balance work and marriage or family at some time (Farber, 1996). They may

delay a career to pursue family or delay a family to pursue career, but some will attempt

to have both at once (Cinamon, 2006; Hakim, 2006; McCracken & Weitzman, 1997). Yet

women's career choices are often constrained by the often-cited biological clock. In

short, a female's ability to procreate ends at an earlier age than does a male's. This

obvious physical difference creates some less-obvious differences in the sociological and psychological forces operating on women and men in the workplace (Impett, Gable, & Peplau, 2005; Rothbard, 2001; Voydanoff & Donnelly, 1989).

There is a growing realization that women's need for achievement reflects both careerist and maternal motivations (McCracken & Weitzman, 1997; Spitze, 1988; Warner, Winter, & Breshears, 2005). Some studies indicate that when women enter the work force, their ability to focus on family and home life is compromised (McElwain, Korabik, & Rosin, 2005; Rothbard, 2001). One limitation of these studies is that they explore a diverse range of workers, from those who must work to support themselves to those who work to enrich their lives. Moreover, many studies combine men and women, who may have different requirements for their balance of roles (Adams, King, & King, 1996; Davis, Spencer, & Steele, 2005; Wentling, 1998).

Hochschild's (1997) study of a Fortune 500 company documented a shift: More women described work, instead of home, as a haven. Women want to work, and they respond positively to the work environment, seeing it as a break from the domestic and child-rearing tasks of home. From 1990-1993, Hochschild interviewed 150 people in middle and top management positions, finding that men and women responded differently to the demands of work and home. Men viewed work as an opportunity to develop self-esteem through financial independence. Women viewed work as a way to increase their self-esteem through expression of themselves. Hochschild concluded that many career women see work as an enhancement to their family life. However, this conclusion has been challenged by other studies that indicate work is an impediment to family life (Jones, Burke, & Westman, 2006; Schneider & Waite, 2005). As women rise to higher levels in management, they find they are spending more hours at work and fewer hours at home. Many of these women say it is too difficult to balance work with home, and the attempt causes stress in the home (Kiecolt, 2003).

Executive women have the proven skills to succeed in business, yet there is still a question about the emotional costs resulting from conflicts between work and personal life. Asking executive women about work and family balance sheds new light on the emotional costs of such an attempt. Women work for many reasons: financial need, providing supplemental family income, self-esteem, and personal satisfaction (Parasuraman & Greenhaus, 1999). Holahan and Gilbert (1979) divided women into those who saw work as a career and those who viewed it as a job, that is, primarily a financial necessity. The women working for a job had a higher incidence of role conflict than did the career women. Executive women, on the other hand, were less likely to feel required to work for economic reasons because they had reached financial security. They may be motivated more by self-fulfillment and satisfaction than by financial exigency. It is important to learn more about why such women work and how they perceive the tradeoffs that their careers have necessitated.

Instead of tradeoffs, Burke (2004) emphasized the integration of work and family over time instead of the 50-50 view of work and family as separate entities. Burke assumed that integration manifests itself differently at different times of life, with the focus shifting from work to family or family to work based on current life conditions. Executive women, who typically have achieved considerable career success, represent a fruitful topic of study regarding the changing dynamics of work and family demands.

A major theme for career women emerges from the literature on the workplace: breaking the glass ceiling influences the differential time demands experienced by women. Occupational success may require more time on the job for women than for men. This time allocation may be self-imposed or result from differences in background and experience necessary to obtain management roles (Goren, 2003; Kirchmeyer, 2002; Ragins & Cotton, 1999). However, one factor complicating an understanding of women's shifting attitudes toward work and home is the tendency to lump all women in the workplace together: hourly workers, part-time employees, middle- and upper-management careers. The focus of this study, executive women, represents a subset of career men and women. The next logical step is to ask executive women if career has been an enhancement or an impediment to their relationships in marriage and family. An increase in executive women leaving their careers to focus on home may reflect this change. Others may be focusing on career and opting out of marriage and children.

Executive Women: Opting Out or Changing Direction?

Hewlett and Luce (2005) noted an increase in the number of highly placed women leaving the corporate world and pursuing self-employment. This trend is a concern for the companies that train and promote women, only to have them leave when they reach the upper echelons of management. Most of these women never reenter the work force at the same level. Some start their own company (women own the majority of new small businesses) or return to work part-time or in a lower paying position. However, other researchers have reached different conclusions. Lyness and Judiesch (2001) found that executive women who were promoted in the last year were less likely than men to voluntarily leave their position. In summary, there is a gap in the literature on executive women and the rationale for their career decisions.

Theoretical Underpinnings

Historically, theoretical attempts to explain career and family issues have focused on variations of work and family roles and conflict in these roles. The three theories relevant to this study are role theory, role conflict theory, and spillover theory. All three are based on the assumption of conflict, which predicts that work demands will strain the family relationship (Heller & Watson, 2005; McCracken & Weitzman, 1997). Role theory links work and family conflict to the time spent in each domain (Greenhaus & Beutell, 1985; Greenhaus & Parasuraman, 1986; Greenhaus et al., 2001). Role conflict theory predicts that women will experience conflict in combining career and family (Greenhaus & Butell, 1985; Greenhaus et al, 2001; Netemeyer, Boles, & McMurrian, 1996). Spillover theory expands that notion by distinguishing between enhancement and conflict (Mennino & Rubin, 2005), suggesting that skill sets in one realm enhance those in the other (Hanson et al., 2006). Spillover theory indicates that work can be both an enhancement (opportunity) and a conflict (loss) to family life (Kiecolt, 2003; Kossek & Ozeki, 1998; McElwain, Korabik, & Rosin 2005).

Role Theory

Role theory addresses the personal conflict of performing a role and meeting the demands of different roles such as employee, spouse, and parent. Role theory takes into account the expectations of society in those roles. It describes interactions of individuals with their social environment in specific settings.

Role theory focuses on traditional gender roles (Impett et al., 2005; Voydanoff & Donnelly, 1989). For example, many studies have found that women assume more domestic and child-rearing responsibilities than males do and that women struggle more with maternal instincts and guilt feelings regarding their family roles (Farber, 1996; Hochschild, 1997; Hyde et al., 1998). Although both men and women state a desire to balance career and family, the burden of fulfilling child care responsibilities tends to fall disproportionately on women (Buffardi, Smith, O'Brien, & Erdwins, 1999; Burke, 2004; Kiecolt, 2003). Role theory is based on evolutionary theory, which imputes to women a primal need for stability and security in intimacy prior to procreation, and in their absence women may choose not to procreate (Archer, 1996).

Executive women may still exhibit the concerns predicted by role theory, which might be manifest in their choices regarding marriage and children. Executive women as an employment group need to be examined to see if they have the same concerns for roles and societal expectations that are predicted by role theory. Women still face obstacles in business, yet the question of whether that reflects self-imposed, career-imposed, or societal limitations continues to be debated. Existing research fails to indicate how women make decisions to balance work and family. Only a qualitative study can ask women what choices they have made and how these have affected their balance of work and family life. The next logical question to ask is the extent to which executive women's work and family choices have been based on maternal instincts and nurturing, and losses or opportunities.

Role Conflict Theory

Role conflict theory follows the framework of role theory but emphasizes work-family conflict, both work-to-family and family-to-work (Greenhaus & Beutell, 1985; Greenhaus et al., 2001; Netemeyer, Boles, & McMurrian, 1996). Along with work-family conflict is the conflicting variable of role strain, which results from competing expectations of one role over another, the internal stress of a role, and the time constraints of roles (Steenbergen, Ellemers, & Mooijaart, 2007). Steenbergen et al. found that women in particular are subject to role conflict and strain; they often have guilt feelings over the relationship among wife, mother, and work roles. According to role conflict theory, one role must take precedence over others; one role is draining and depletes the energy required to focus on another role. Conflict theory assumes that work and family priorities are in conflict. For example, an increase in the work role correlates to a depletion of resources for the family role.

A longitudinal study of talented female students found that they faced two main challenges: career goals and family goals. The conflict women experience in making choices regarding career and family is reflected in the attitudes of young girls. Young people say that balancing careers and family is important for both men and women. Yet girls begin worrying about that balance at a younger age than do boys (Perrone, Civiletto, Webb, & Fitch, 2004). Men tend to think a career is attainable with family, whereas women anticipate more conflict between the two (Tinklin, Croxford, Ducklin, & Frame, 2005). McCracken and Weitzman (1997) found that women were waiting longer to get married and have a family if they first pursued a career right after college. Hakim (2006) found that work takes priority over family and social life for professional women, and half the women in professional positions are childless and many have married more than once.

Literature on work-to-family conflict and family-to-work conflict indicates that both influence job-life satisfaction (Higgins et al., 2001). In a meta-analysis, Kossek and Ozeki (1998) considered work-to-family conflict as it relates to job-life satisfaction. They found that people with high levels of conflict are less satisfied with their jobs. They also found that whereas work conflict was related to job satisfaction, family influence was unrelated to job satisfaction. There was a negative relationship of work-to-family conflict for dual-career families. The reciprocal influences of work and family can be positive, negative, or neutral, which could account for the differences in variables used in quantitative surveys that address how job affects family life (Friedman & Greenhaus, 2000).

Spillover Theory

The ability to have high satisfaction in both home and work is based on the spillover theory that skill sets in one realm enhance those in the other (Tiedje et al., 1990). Spillover theory seeks to explain work-family relationships in positive and enhancing ways as well as negative or conflicting ways (Grandey, Cordeiro, & Crouter, 2005; Hanson, Hammer, & Colton, 2006; Impett et al., 2005; Kossek & Ozeki, 1998). The notion of work as an enhancement to family instead of a conflict is a fairly recent research hypothesis (Jackson & Scharman, 2002; Jones, Braithwaite, & Healy, 2003; Kiecolt, 2003). The enhancement hypothesis is sometimes defined as the reverse of the conflict hypothesis (Grandey et al., 2005; Hanson, Hammer, & Colton, 2006). The enhancement hypothesis suggests that the demands of career and family, rather than depleting one another, can increase energy and self-esteem. Here, family and work environments complement each other, enhancing performance in both realms. The enhancement hypothesis predicts that women with a career will have success in marriage and with children due to positive spillover from work (Hammer, Cullen, Neal, Sinclair, & Shafico, 2005).

A qualitative study of career public accountants found that they dealt effectively with conflict without disturbing either work or family life. The majority accepted demands on the job and were able to benefit from the rewards of money and prestige. When the woman's career resulted in improved family finances, there was less conflict for her spouse (Greenhaus, Parasuraman, & Collins, 2001). Greenhaus et al. found a difference between those who worked to support their family and those who described work as a career, in other words, between low career involvement (those who had to work) and high career involvement (those who worked to have a career). Most single mothers and women who needed to support the family found little benefit to work beyond meeting financial needs. Career women, on the other hand, tolerated work interference to obtain the benefits of a high-level position. Greenhaus et al. found that positive mental states reciprocated in work and marriage. This finding parallels other studies on how positive attitudes enrich and negative attitudes deplete the spillover of work and family (Heller & Watson, 2005; Impett, Gable, & Peplau, 2005).

High Conflict Versus High Enhancement

Role theory, role conflict theory, and spillover theory have considered work and family as either in conflict with each other or an enhancement to each other. It may be that both can occur, as suggested by Tiedje et al. (1990), who interviewed 200 professional women to develop a scale of perceptions of role conflict or enhancement. They found that neither role conflict nor role enhancement adequately explained the attempt to balance roles. Participants said they did not perceive conflict and enhancement at opposite ends of the spectrum. Instead, the women exhibited both conflict and enhancement at different times in their lives, and balancing the two was critical. It was that balance that predicted life satisfaction. The women with high conflict and high enhancement were happier and better able to cope than were those rated as low conflict and low enhancement. Tiedje et al. also suggested that personality and coping skills influence the decision to take on multiple roles and responsibilities.

There is no clear indication of how the three theories summarized above apply to executive women. Role theory, which is based on evolutionary theory, assumes traditional roles for women (Impett et al., 2005; Voydanoff & Donnelly, 1989). It separates the roles of employee and mother and fails to consider how the roles can interact positively. Role conflict theory assumes that competing role expectations cause conflict because women take on nurturing and maternal roles at home and feel guilty when they are at work. This theory assumes that the conflict is draining and women must choose which role has precedence: work or family (Marks, 1977; Tinklin et al., 2005). Spillover theory, on the other hand, assumes that work can be a positive influence on home life (Frone et al., 1992; Jackson & Scharman, 2002; Jones et al., 2003). The high conflict versus high enhancement perspective suggests that career is both an opportunity and a conflict to family at different times (Tiedje et al., 1990). It is unclear which theory best explains the lived experiences of executive women who are working full-time. The next logical step is to ask executive women to discuss whether their career has been an opportunity, an impediment, or both at various times and how they handled the stages.

Summary

Women have made significant inroads into the business world, yet at what cost? It is important to study the accomplishments of executive women and their attempts to balance career with home life. Such a study was needed because the literature on balancing career and family life does not adequately portray the experiences of executive women. Research has documented a difference between career and noncareer women and their balance of work and family. Theories have variously assumed that home and work are inherently in conflict, or that they can enhance each other (Frone et al., 1992; Grandey et al., 2005; Greenhaus & Beutell, 1985; Greenhaus et al., 2001; Impett et al., 2005; Netemeyer et al., 1996; Tiedje et al, 1990; Voydanoff & Donnelly, 1989). Research indicates that women experience self-esteem, rewards, and satisfaction from careers. Work increases empowerment, and this leads to greater life satisfaction and reduces psychological problems (Hyde, DeLamter, & Durik, 2001).

There is an extensive literature on the relationship between work and family and the effects of gender on leadership skills. Current theories focus on work-family balance as either conflict (loss) or an enhancement (opportunity) to each other. The high conflict verse high enhancement perspective has suggested that both dynamics can occur at different times in one's life (Tiedje et al., 1990). There is a gap in the research on executive women, who may or may not experience the same role conflicts or opportunities as other groups. Executive women may have tried to balance work and family, or they may have chosen between the two. This study of executive women attempted to discover themes or patterns in the choices participants have made to balance career, marriage, and family. Individual interviews explored the dynamics of those choices.

This chapter reviewed the relevant research for a qualitative study on how executive women attempt to balance work and family. It recounted the influence of the feminist movement on women's career options. It reviewed women's efforts to balance their career goals with their family responsibilities. It evaluated the appropriateness of role theory, role conflict theory, and spillover theory to explain those efforts, and it considered the merits of examining executive women's experience as characterized by high conflict or high enhancement. Chapter 3 will describe the study's methods, including the rationale, sample, data collection and analysis, and the ethical protection of participants.

CHAPTER 3: RESEARCH METHODS

Introduction

This research studied executive women, defined as women who were over 35 years old who have held supervisory positions and have achieved significant influence and financial success. Executive women are an emerging group because it has taken the last 10-20 years for them to advance up in the corporate world. Their ranks include CEOs, presidents, vice presidents, managers, and supervisors. The study began gathering data only after receiving approval from the University Institutional Research Board (IRB study number 11-07-98-0283569) to proceed. The goal of this study was to understand executive women group through a qualitative study that asked how career affects choices regarding marriage and children. The qualitative study, based on the phenomenological approach, used open-ended interviews to engage participants in a conversation about their attempts to balance career with marriage and children. The goal was to prompt participants to discuss their journey to a career and the effects on balancing other dimensions of their lives along the way.

Research Questions

This study was guided by three research questions:

1. How have executive women made choices about careers, and how have those decisions affected the way they balance marriage and children?

2. How have career choices been an opportunity (enhancement) or loss (conflict) regarding marriage and children?

3. What sacrifices have executive women made in pursuing a career, and what regrets do they have, if any?

These questions were based on the conflict and enhancement perspectives of the spillover and role theories. The conflict perspective predicts that career will cause conflict and result in negative repercussions for family life. Work demands will strain family life and force a choice between career and family. Some studies have indicated that when women enter the work force, their ability to focus on family and home life is compromised. Work, then, represents a conflict (loss) with respect to family life (McElwain, Korabik, & Rosin, 2005; Rothbard, 2001).

Conversely, the enhancement perspective predicts that career will be an enhancement (opportunity) to family life by creating a positive spillover (Frone et al., 1992; Jackson & Scharman, 2002; Jones, Braithwaite, & Healy, 2003; Kiecolt, 2003; Tiedje et al., 1990). Some studies have found that high conflict and high enhancement are an indication of multiple roles that can be balanced depending on the influence of spouse, children, parents, and friends. Tiedje et al. found that women with high conflict and high enhancement were happier and better able to cope than were those rated as low conflict and low enhancement. The researchers also suggested that personality and coping skills influence the decision to take on multiple roles and responsibilities.

Qualitative Method: Phenomenology

The qualitative method explores human experiences to obtain an in-depth understanding of a phenomenon (Moustakas, 1994). Qualitative methods are used to understand the dynamics behind phenomena that do not lend themselves to statistical analysis. They are also used to obtain information when there is a gap in the literature on a specific group. A qualitative study is conducted when a researcher wants to answer questions of how or what. It explores a topic when there is no easy way to obtain variables for a quantitative study (Creswell, 2007; Moustakas, 1994; Wolcott, 2001).

A qualitative study facilitates the discovery of rationales and a more detailed history or explanation of a certain group (Creswell, 2007). Qualitative designs are well-suited to exploring the process of a new and emerging group, which was the focus of the current study on the lived experiences of executive women. The phenomenological approach focuses on the conscious awareness and knowledge of the essence of an experience. It explores the meaning and details of a phenomenon that are difficult to convey in a quantitative study (Creswell, 2007; Moustakas, 1994; Wolcott, 2001).

Quantitative research may explore such variables as self-esteem, mental health, and life satisfaction yet fail to describe the life experiences of women struggling to balance and integrate the various parts of their personal and professional lives. The goal of this qualitative study was to capture the struggles of achieving career success and the potential tradeoffs regarding marriage and children. The dynamics of career are difficult to portray in a purely quantitative approach, which tends to focus on a narrow slice of time. As such, qualitative methods provide explanations for phenomena such as career and home life over an extended period of time (Schensul, Schensul, & LeCompte, 1999).

Of the five qualitative approaches, both the phenomenological approach and the grounded approach are appropriate for an interview-based study. The phenomenological approach was chosen over the grounded approach because the primary goal of this study was to see if current theories of work and family balance (role theory, role conflict theory and spillover theory) apply to executive women. The grounded approach focuses on the process of generating substantive theory. The phenomenological approach focuses on describing experiences and their meaning (Creswell, 2007). This qualitative study used the theory of phenomenology to develop themes of executive women who were among the few to focus on moving up the corporate ladder to succeed in earning management positions while integrating family as a normal process in their life. Phenomenology facilitates an extensive study of a small number of participants to obtain an in-depth understanding of their unique experiences. This study used the tenets of role theory, role conflict theory, and spillover theory to explore the concepts of conflict (losses) and enhancement (opportunities) in participants' lives. Individual interviews were based on Moustakas's (1994) notion of transcendental or psychological phenomenology and analyzed executive women's experiences to develop an understanding of their individual and shared experiences.

Rationale for Study

The qualitative method was a good fit for the proposed study because a review of the literature indicated there are few studies that target executive women, a group that needs to be explored in light of their life choices (Creswell, 2007). The goal was to discover participants' perceptions about their career: how they chose their given path and how their career choices affected decisions about marriage and children. A qualitative approach was chosen to address the gap in the literature regarding the life choices of executive women and their attempts to balance career with marriage and children. A qualitative approach was selected as the methodology most appropriate for exploring the lived experiences of executive women.

Interviews provide a richer description of participants' lived experience than would a quantitative survey. Qualitative research can complement quantitative research by discovering attitudes and opinions of participants. In this study, qualitative research was necessary due to the limited information in the research literature about executive women. Most quantitative studies to date have combined many occupational groups: men and women with all levels of work experience, education, and financial needs for work. Many quantitative studies on careers have focused on college students (Adams, King, & King, 1996; Cinamon, 2006; Perrone et al., 2004; Perrone & Worthington, 2001; Rothbard, 2001). The perceptions of college students may have little to say about the experiences of executive women.

Quantitative studies have considered a variety of occupations: full-time workers at a university (Holahan & Gilbert, 1978), public utility and customer service employees (Hanson et al., 2006), dual income workers; wife and husband (Hyde et al., 1998), and certified public accountants (Greenhaus et al., 2001). Qualitative studies have tended to focus on groups that include men and women at different levels of work experience or income (Johnson-Bailey & Tisdell, 1998), including working mothers with flexible schedules (Jackson & Schaman, 2002), parents raising children and working at least 10 hours a week (Grandey et al., 2005), and managers at a leadership seminar (Graves et al., 2007).

The quantitative and qualitative literature does reveal some common themes. Some studies, for example indicate women have more conflict between career and family than do men (Freidman & Greenhaus, 2000; Graves et al., 2007; Hanson et al., 2006; Jones et al., 2006; Lyness & Judiesch, 2001; Perrone et al., 2004; Schneider & Waite, 2005). Others suggest that women assume more domestic and child-rearing responsibilities than males do and that women struggle more with maternal instincts and guilt feelings regarding their family roles (Farber, 1996; Hochschild, 1997; Hyde et al.,

1998). Studies suggest that women enjoy working for esteem and confidence

(Hochschild, 1997; Holahan & Gilbert, 1979; Kiecolt, 2003); career women are more

independent and aggressive, which may conflict with spouse and family (Abele, 2003;

Berdahl & Anderson; 2005; Hyde; 2005; Maroda, 2004); and career women often delay

marriage and family (Cinamon, 2006; Hakim, 2006; McCracken & Weitzman, 1997).

Current theories focus on work-family balance as either conflict (loss) or an

enhancement (opportunity) to each other. There is a gap in the research on executive

women, who may or may not experience the same role conflicts or opportunities as other

groups. The goal of this dissertation study was to discover themes that shed light on the

life experiences of executive women and how their career choices affect decisions of

marriage and children. The opportunity to tell their own stories personalized the results

and provided deeper insight into this unique group of women than would a quantitative

approach. It is suggested when there is a gap in the literature there is a benefit to proceed

with thorough in-depth interviews to allow the group to reflect on their experiences and

choices (Moustakas, 1994).

Sample and Sampling Procedure

This study used criterion and convenience sampling strategies appropriate to

qualitative inquiry. The sampling for a phenomenological study has a narrow focus. It

was necessary for all participants to have experienced the same phenomenon (Creswell,

2007, p. 128). Sampling for the current study selected executive women, defined as those

women over 35 years who have held supervisory positions in management and leadership

roles in business for at least 10 years. Executive women have carved a path into upper management that requires extensive hours and often offers little flexibility. Typical executive women have responsibilities (e.g., extended work hours, work emergencies, travel) that differ from women engaged in professional services. They include CEOs, presidents, vice presidents, managers, and supervisors.

A convenience sample was based on the researcher's business contacts and ability to tap a wide market of executive women. The researcher did not use her own current or potential clients. In keeping with Creswell's (2007) recommendation, participants were selected; all came from the southwest region of the United States. Member checking was conducted, and some additional executive women not part of interviews were asked to check the results and see if they were applicable to them. Saturation was determined when the transcripts indicated consistent and reoccurring common themes for this group. The study found saturation was accomplished with 10 participants to develop consensus of general themes or patterns. Saturation was determined by the researcher after the initial 10 interviews were completed and it was determined there were sufficient data to code and formulate the emergent themes. Criterion sampling included a short list of questions to make sure potential participants were in a supervisory role, had at least 10 years experience in their industry, and had moved up the ladder in their company.

Data Collection

This study addressed a gap in the literature on executive women by exploring their experiences of conflict (loss) and enhancement (opportunity) in career and family life. Interviews addressed the lived experience of executive women and how choices about career affected the balance of marriage and family life. As a qualitative study, it was retrospective, in contrast to a quantitative study, which only assesses

attitudes at the time a survey is completed.

Each interview was conducted in either the participant's or researcher's

office, as mutually acceptable and convenient for the participant. The interviews were

informal and lasted an average of 60 minutes. Additional participant interviews were

conducted when necessary to validate and confirm concepts. The researcher conducted the

informal interviews and asked each participant explain what she had experienced in her

career as it related to choices, including sacrifices, regarding marriage, children, and

family life.

Interviews were recorded on audiotape for transcription by the researcher and input into

Nvivo 8 software. A short survey administered prior to the interview and notes

determined if the participant was single, married, or divorced, and whether she had

children.

The following lettered interview questions were used to explore the study's main

research questions (numbered).

1. How have executive women made choices about careers, and how have those
decisions affected the way they balance marriage and children?

a. Can you give a general outline of how you proceeded with your career and the
decisions you made in the process regarding marriage and children?

b. Did you think about marriage and children before embarking on your   career?

-At what point in your career did you begin pondering decisions about
family?

-Did you delay one over the other? Why and how did you make
that decision

c. What factors did you consider in making your choices?

d. Whom did you seek out for advice and support?

e. Who was instrumental in influencing your decisions?

2. How have career choices been an opportunity (enhancement) or loss (conflict) regarding marriage and children? What sacrifices have executive women made in pursuing a career, and what regrets do they have?

a. What opportunities and losses have been associated with your career?

b. What happened to open up opportunities for you? Was it planned?

c. Give an example of a positive opportunity in your life. What losses do you remember as significant in your life?

d. What changes have you made in your work to accommodate marriage and children?

e. Do you consider these changes a sacrifice?

f. Would you make changes or sacrifices in the future for the sake of marriage and children?

Data Analysis

Phenomenology was used as the researcher focused on executive women and how their career choices affect the attempt to balance marriage and family life. A reflective process was defined by Moustakas (1994) as a way "to provide a logical, systematic, and coherent resource for carrying out the analysis and synthesis needed to arrive at essential descriptions of experience" (p. 47). The reflective process allowed participants to describe their experience using feelings, thoughts, and examples. After the interviews were completed and transcribed, the researcher coded the transcriptions to observe

patterns and themes. Coding was employed using a modification of the

Stevick-Colaizzi-Keen method of analysis developed by Moustakas, who

listed the steps of that method as follows:

From the verbatim transcripts complete the following steps:

1. Consider the statement with respect to significance for description of

   experience.

2. Record all relevant statements.

3. List nonrepetitive, nonoverlapping statements. These are the invariant
horizons of meaning units of the experience.

4. Relate and cluster the invariant meaning units into themes.

5. Synthesize the invariant meaning units and themes in a description of the
textures of the experience. Use examples.

6. Through imaginative variation, construct a description of the structures
of the experience.

7. Construct textural-structural descriptions of the meanings and essences
of the experience.

8. The researcher completed these steps for herself, which helped her be
aware of her experiences by viewing them in written form, thus exposing her bias
on the subject.

Successful data collection depended on the researcher's ability to establish

relationships and gain the trust of participants. The researcher reviewed the

audio transcipts to construct textural-structural descriptions that revealed the

meanings and essence of participants' experiences. Steps 1-7, listed above, were

followed for each participant to

develop common themes and meanings explained in the findings. Individual results were combined to create a composite textural-structural description representing the group as a whole.

After the transcribed data were analyzed using the Stevick-Colaizzi-Keen method described above, data were entered into the NVivo 8 qualitative software package. This procedure supplemented hand coding to allow themes to emerge from the data. NVivo 8 identified common words and themes, and confirmed the data as relevant or irrelevant to this subgroup of executive women. Coding reflected how participants' careers affected decisions in the areas of marriage, children, and family life, both opportunities (positive statements) and losses (negative statements).

The data reflected the emic process of participants clarifying their everyday experience of becoming executive women and their life choices regarding marriage and family (Wolcott, 1994). Qualitative research allows in-depth study of specific executive women to gain more information than is currently available about this important occupational group. The study was based on Moustakas's (1994) transcendental or psychological phenomenology. By bracketing her own experience and interpreting participants' experiences, the researcher sought fresh perspectives on the pursuit of career leadership and the attempt to balance career and family. This provided an emic view of the participants, whereas the researcher, because of her experience in the business world, had an epic view of the topic. The researcher documented her experience and was open to new interpretations and the emergence of novel themes.

The researcher needed to continually analyze and revise data with each interview.

This process enhanced the development of cohesive themes. Moustakas (1994) described

four steps in the phenomenological process: epoche, phenomenological reduction,
imaginative variation, and synthesis of composite textural and structural

descriptions (pp.180-181). Epoche is the ability of the researcher to set aside

prejudgments and remain unbiased and open to participants' experiences. Using

the Stevick-Colaizzi-Keen method analysis helps a researcher remain objective

in data analysis and coding. By being aware of one's etic knowledge, a

researcher is able to better acknowledge his or her beliefs on the subject at hand.

Phenomenological reduction consists of bracketing thetopic and horizontalizing

or clustering the meanings into invariant qualities and themes.

The goal is to cluster themes so they accurately reflect the group's shared

experience (Creswell, 2007).

In the present study, emergent themes were first coded as opportunities

or losses,based on the spillover and role conflict theory as they relate to family

life and career. A second coding considered other influences that were

consistent among participants, which involved an inductive coding scheme.

Imaginative variation is a synthesis of the interview results designed to

determine how intentional and conscious participants were in charting their

career paths. The final step was organizing, analyzing, and synthesizing data

using the Stevick-Colaizzi-Keen method and NVivo 8 qualitative software to

develop individual and composite descriptions, leading to themes representing the essence of participants' experience (Moustakas, 1994). When the researcher noticed

redundancies in interviews, that was an indication saturation had been achieved

(LeCompte & Schensul, 1999; Nastasi & Schensul, 2005). The researcher used "inductive

data analysis to review the interviews and stop when redundancy of meaning (in data,

constructs, and theory) occurred also referred to as data saturation" (Nastasi & Schensul,

38, 2005, p. 9). Discrepant Cases will be described in Chapter 4 by pie charts and

description as well as explanation of discrepancy found during the interviews.

Verification and Trustworthiness

Trustworthiness is confidence in the results of a study; it reflects the reliability

and validity of research instruments. To insure trustworthiness, the study included

triangulation, peer debriefing, member checks, an audit trail, and referential adequacy

(Lincoln & Guba, 1985). The sampling ensured persistent observation as needed with

other executive women. Triangulation was achieved by interpreting interview results in

light of current theory. Referential adequacy was accomplished by archiving audio

recordings so the researcher could obtain raw data for analysis and interpretation to verify

conclusions. The researcher used observation as well as Nivo 8 software to determine

themes and separate relevant factors from irrelevant factors (Lincoln & Guba, 1985,

Nastasi & Schensul, 2005). Verification was determined through data input and analysis

of the results to develop common themes.

Member checking was used by asking participants to verify themes as an accurate

reflection of their experience. Member checking also involved other executive women

who were not interviewed. They were asked to comment on the relevance for their own lives of the themes identified in the study. Member checking and peer debriefing enhance

credibility and internal validity of a qualitative study. Peer debriefing involved

psychology professionals who reviewed the researcher's coding. An audit trail was

accomplished by archiving audio recordings and the researcher's notes from the

interviews (Lincoln & Guba, 1985; Nastasi & Schensul, 2005).

The goal was to ensure that findings were an accurate representation of participants' expressions.

The researcher's knowledge of the subject was based on her own experience as an

executive woman for over 20 years and her knowledge of the occupational culture of

executive women, which helped her gain participants' trust.

Ethics and Confidentiality

The researcher maintained the highest ethical principals throughout the study.

Participants signed a consent form (Appendix A) that guaranteed the confidentiality and

anonymity of interviews. The consent form included information on the purpose of the

study, participant criteria, confidentiality and anonymity precautions, and procedures for

the interview process. Participants were informed that participation was voluntary and

could be discontinued at any time. The purpose of the study, why the participant was

selected, and the time frame and participation requirements were made clear. Due to the

career positions of some participants, pseudonyms were used in reporting information.

Revealing quotations or other potentially identifying features were eliminated or

paraphrased.

Interviews were audio taped, and tapes were offered to participants upon

completion of the study. Any audiotapes not returned will be locked in a safety deposit box for 5 years. Any electronic data compiled while completing the research will be password protected, and no direct identifiers such as names, addresses, or telephone numbers will be revealed. No code numbers linked to specific persons will be revealed to any person other than the researcher. No participants were current or prior clients or employers of the research

Summary

This chapter described the methods for a qualitative study on how executive women attempt to balance work and family. It summarized the study's rationale, sample, data collection, and data analysis. It also described steps taken to preserve participants' anonymity and the confidentiality of their interview responses. The next chapter summarizes the study's results.

CHAPTER 4: FINDINGS

Introduction

This chapter summarizes the findings of a qualitative study based on individual interviews with executive women from the southwestern United States. Interviews were conducted from December 2008 to April 2009 and were held in participants' offices. The phenomenological approach involved open-ended questions to engage participants in conversations to describe their experiences in pursuing a career while balancing marriage and children. All interviews were audio recorded.

The researcher listened to the audio recordings immediately after the interviews to make notes and transcribe the interviews into a Microsoft Word file (see Appendix C). The researcher followed the Stevick-Colaizzi-Keen method, as summarized by Moustakas (1994), to develop meanings and themes. Consistent categories were developed with distinct titles and subtitles, and the data were manually coded with these categories. The NVivo 8 qualitative software package was then used to further analyze the data and confirm emergent themes, identify nonconforming data, and generate charts and graphs. After the interviews were completed and transcribed, the researcher coded the transcriptions to observe patterns and themes. Coding was employed using a modification of the Stevick-Colaizzi-Keen method of analysis developed by Moustakas, who listed the steps of that method as follows:

From the verbatim transcripts complete the following steps:

1. Consider the statement with respect to significance for description of experience.

2. Record all relevant statements.

3. List nonrepetitive, nonoverlapping statements. These are the invariant horizons of meaning units of the experience.

4. Relate and cluster the invariant meaning units into themes.

5. Synthesize the invariant meaning units and themes in a description of the textures of the experience. Use examples.

6. Through imaginative variation, construct a description of the structures of the experience.

7. Construct textural-structural descriptions of the meanings and essences of the experience. (Moustakas, 1994, p.122)

The researcher approached this study as a woman in the business world. She had her own biases regarding how she predicted the turnout of the results of the study. The details of her biases are presented in the results section in Chapter 5 titled Researcher's Experience. Successful data collection depended on the researcher's ability to establish relationships and gain the trust of participants. The researcher reviewed the audio transcripts to construct textural-structural descriptions that revealed the meanings and essence of participants' experiences. Steps 1-7, listed above, were followed for each participant to develop common themes and meanings explained in the findings. Individual results were combined to create a composite textural-structural description representing the group as a whole.

After the transcribed data were analyzed using the Stevick-Colaizzi-Keen method described above, data were entered into the NVivo 8 qualitative software package. This procedure allowed themes to emerge from the data. NVivo 8 identified common words and themes, and confirmed the data as relevant or irrelevant to this subgroup of executive women. Coding reflected how participants' careers affected decisions in the

areas of marriage, children and family life both opportunities (positive statements) and

losses (negative statements).

Demographics

Data for this qualitative study were collected through individual

interviews with executive women from a variety of industries in the southwestern United

States: health care, advertising, consumer electronics, broadcast, banking and financial

markets, hospitality, research and pharmaceuticals, hospitals, and retail. Figure 1

summarizes the major types of companies represented by participants.

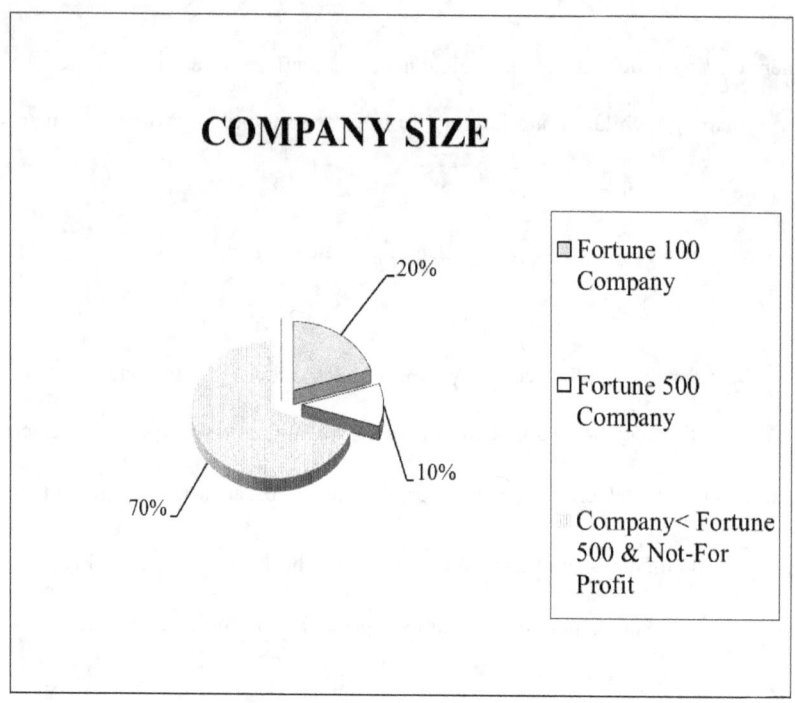

COMPANY SIZE

20%

☐ Fortune 100
Company

☐ Fortune 500
Company

10%

70%

Company< Fortune
500 & Not-For
Profit

Figure 1. Type of company.

One research goal was that the sample included both middle and senior management positions. That goal was achieved, as indicated in Figure 2 below. As a chart, it seems irrelevant to add a pie chart that represents 50% for upper and middle management verses senior management. Yet, it is critical for this study that these women were in the higher echelons of corporate America. These women represent those that pursued their careers while married with children.

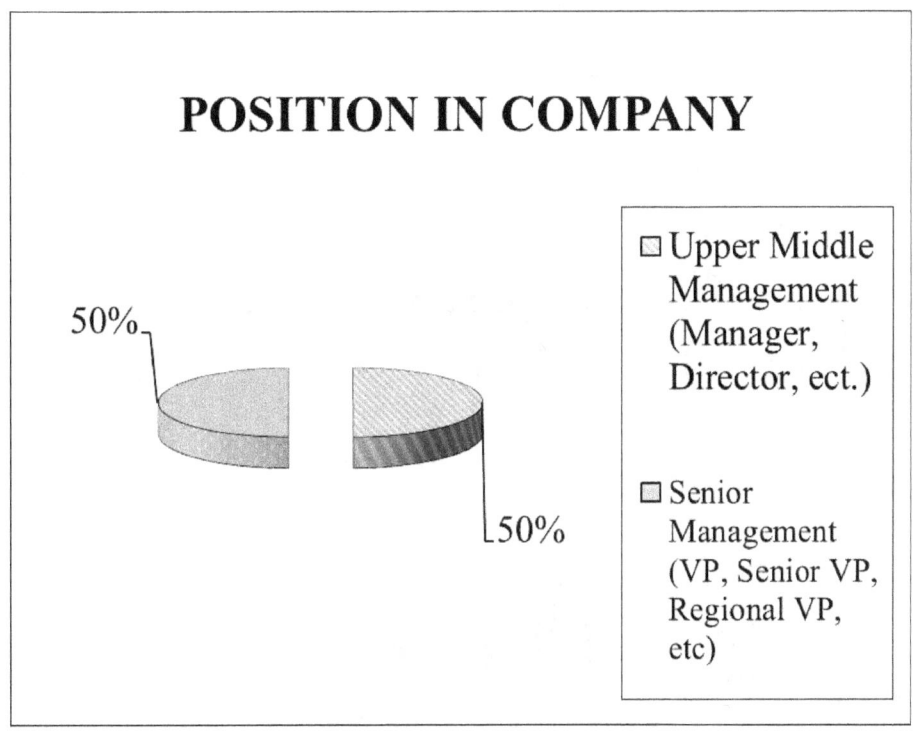

Figure 2. Breakdown of sample by position.

All of the participants were or had been married. Most were married in their 20s and 30s. One discrepant case was a woman who married at 17 and is still married (see Figure 3). These women did not delay marriage due to career. They were advancing in their career while pursuing marriage goals.

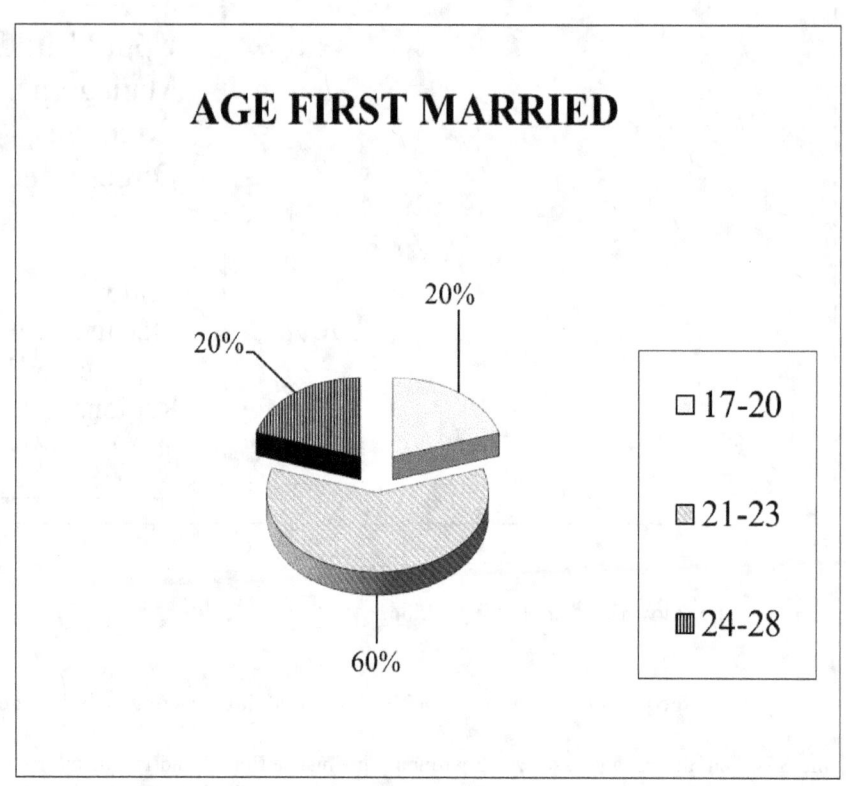

Figure 3. Age when first married.

Most participants had their first child before age 30. One woman was unable to have children, but she helped raise three step-children (see Figure 4). The majority of participants had two or three children (see Figure 5). This indicates there were no delays in waiting to have children due to advancing in their career goals.

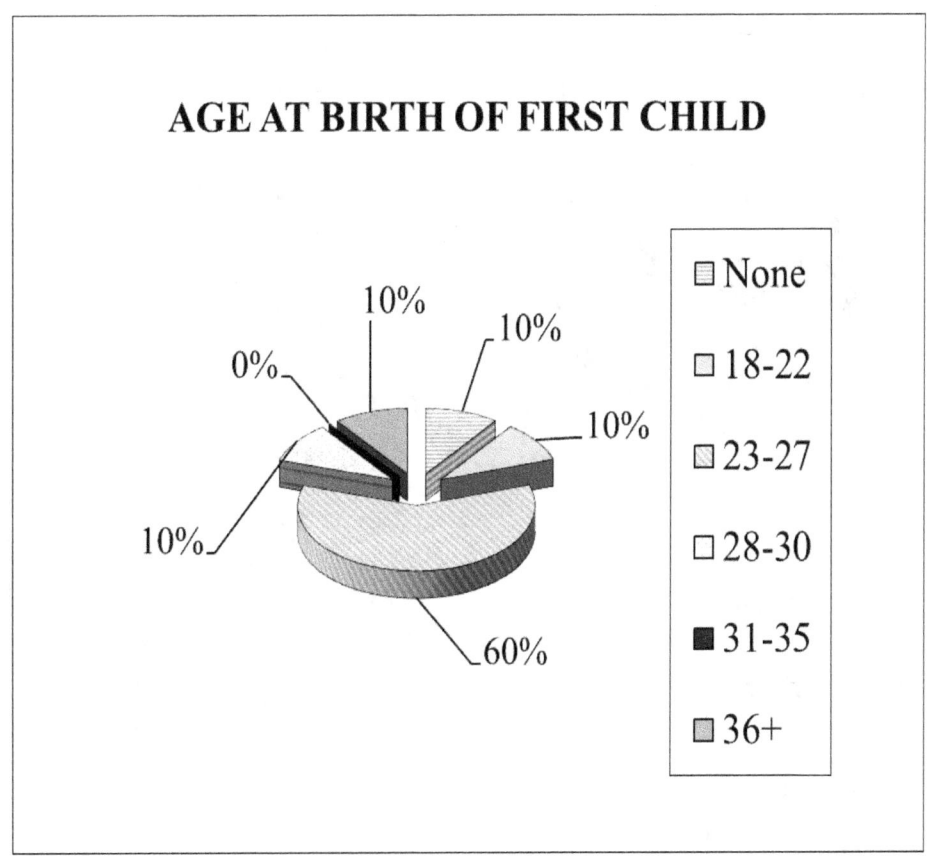

Figure 4. Age at birth of first child

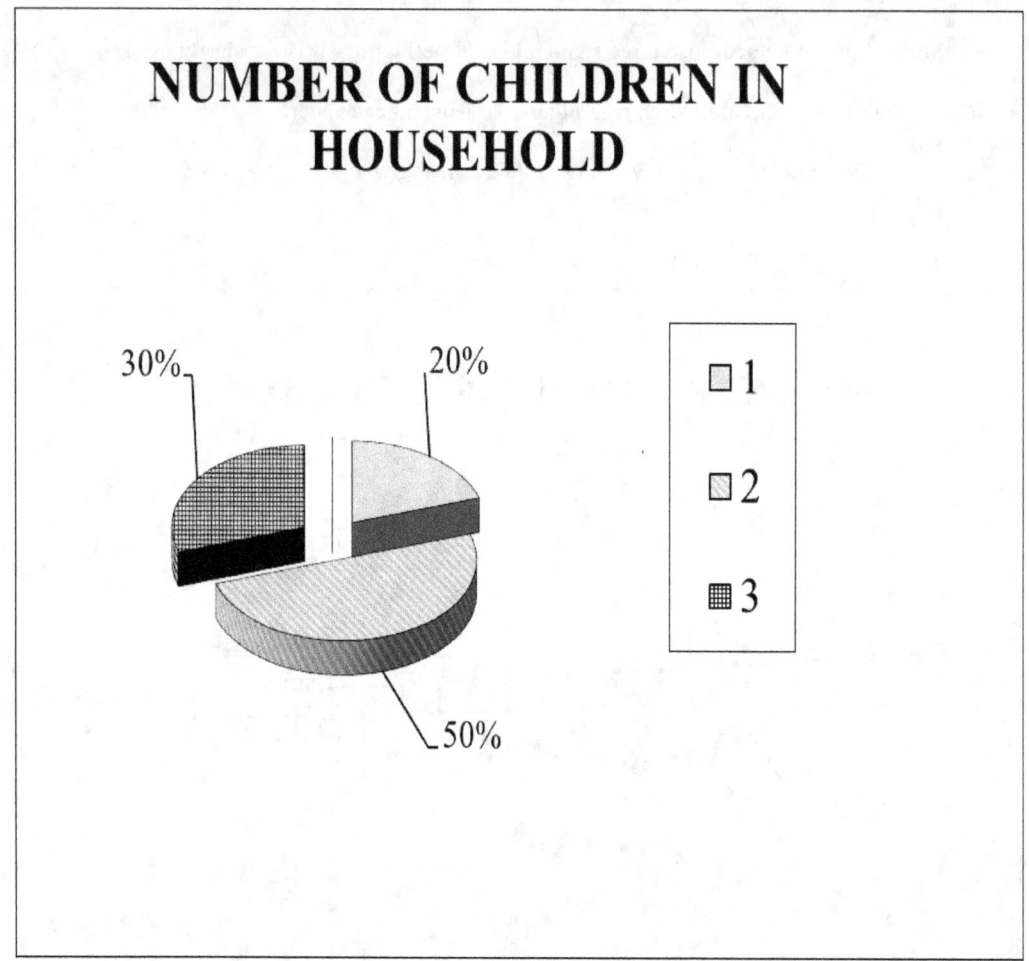

Figure 5. Number of children in household.

Participant Profiles

To retain anonymity, participants were assigned pseudonyms.

Amber is vice president of a nonprofit hospital corporation. She has spent 15 years in the same industry and has been with her current employer for over 10 years. Her industry includes both men and women in management. She completed a master's degree while married, working, and pregnant. She was married at age 30 and assumed she would work and have a career. She is now a single mother and devotes her time to her teenager and her work. She described her career path as follows: "I was good at what I did and I just was promoted. . . . No training or concept of what makes a manager, I just learned. . . . I love what I do at work."

Chloe is national director of sales for an international hotel corporation. She has up to 40 people reporting to her, both men and women, in five states. She has worked in the hotel business for 25 years. She was a single mother with one child for much of her career. She remarried at age 40, when her child was grown.

Hunter is a sales manager at a Fortune 100 consumer electronics and broadcast company. She worked her way up in this company to sales manager. She married her high school sweetheart prior to pursuing a career. She had two children, and she and her husband shared child-rearing responsibilities. She always thought she would have both children and work, and her friends were doing the same thing. She was at the hospital having a baby when she learned she had earned one of her company's highest awards.

Jasmine, vice president of sales for major hospitality corporation, spent 20 years advancing in the hotel industry. When she obtained her current position, she was one of two women in the country in this industry. She married young, was divorced, and then remarried in her early 30s to someone who was in the industry. When she found out she was unable to have her own children, she focused on raising her three stepchildren.

Kayla is an executive producer for an international advertising agency. She has worked in television production and postproduction as well as advertising agencies. She was married and divorced, then remarried in her mid-30s and had a child at age 36. She continued to work while pregnant, and her husband was supportive in sharing responsibilities. She raised two children while balancing her work responsibilities as she moved to top executive in charge of the agency.

Megan, a vice president in commercial banking for a Fortune 100 company, has over 25 years experience in the banking business. She married her college sweetheart, and they both have careers and shared responsibility for raising their two children. She never thought about not working, although at one point she told her boss she would take a 20% cut in salary to work fewer hours and spend more time her children. She ended up working just as many hours as before the pay cut. She later received a promotion.

Nora is sales manager and director for a research corporation that sells tax and legal information. All of the people reporting to her have been men, except one. She met her current husband when she reached the top position in sales at her company. She continued in the same industry and moved into management positions. It was difficult for her to maintain a close relationship with her husband because they often lived in different cities. She has two children and says she did not plan a family or a career. She was in her 30s when she had her first child, and she worked throughout her pregnancy.

Ruby, president of an international health care corporation, was formerly part-owner of a different health care business. She married in her 30s and had two children.

Her husband worked but was not at the same level in his career, which caused difficulties in their marriage. Eventually, they divorced. She described him as "a great father yet not a great husband."

Sophie is director of an international high-end retail corporation. She was married in her 20s and has two children. She obtained a master's degree while raising her children and moving into management positions. She and her husband share child-rearing responsibility. She has been with the same company over 10 years and has continued to move up the corporate ladder.

Violet, sales manager for a Fortune 500 company worked her way up from secretary to executive while pursuing a bachelor's and master's degrees at night and on weekends. She married her high school sweetheart and ended up going to school and working because he traveled and she was lonely. She has two children. Her husband has always been supportive of her goals and career, as well as taking responsibility with the children.

Discrepant Cases

The discrepant cases were discussed in the participant profiles and depicted in the pie charts. The main variation for the participants was the group combined married women, divorced women, single women, women remarried, and with blended families. In addition, there was a variation in the number of children the women were raising from one to four children. There were differences in the support of their husbands with the management of the household and the raising of the children. The revelation was the similarities of the way they approached juggling of domestic and career situations regardless of their marital status or number of children they were raising. These women consistently managed to prioritize and get the job done. Further studies to separate the groups would prove beneficial to observe any discrepancy in their status.

Results

The interviews allowed participants to explain how their career experiences affected marriage and family life. Questions asked how career affected choices regarding marriage and children, and how career has been an opportunity or loss regarding marriage and family life. Opportunities were described by words such as power, pay, prestige, esteem, confidence, control, balance, positive spillover, success, and support from spouse and family. Losses were described as guilt, lack of support from spouse, time constraints, imbalance, and desire to overcome segmentation of roles. Previous studies have found that many successful women experience a sense of loss by delaying marriage and child-rearing, and guilt for neglecting wife and mother roles (Cinamon, 2006; Hakim, 2006; McCracken & Weitzman, 1997). For women who lack a support system from spouse, family, or friends, the time constraints of work may allow little personal or family time, which also contributes to a sense of loss (Davis et al., 2005; Farber, 1996).

Freidman and Greenhaus (2000) discovered a predictive relationship between family and work regarding life satisfaction. When there are two distinct roles (e.g., executive woman and wife or mother), it is possible to have satisfaction in one role and not the other, or in both roles, or in neither. The *happiness domain* is a combination of positive emotions in all domains: career, marriage, and children.

Themes that emerged in the interviews included the following:

1. Participants never seriously entertained the idea of not working.

2. Participants said that career is a positive influence on self.

3. Participants said that career is a positive influence on marriage.

4. Participants said that career is a positive influence on children.

5. Participants said that career responsibilities contribute to maternal guilt.

6. While acknowledging having made sacrifices for their careers, participants did not express regrets.

Results are arranged by research question. Patterns and themes that emerged from the data will be discussed, along with discrepant or noncomforming data, when relevant. Information is not presented in order of importance.

Research Question 1

How have you made choices about career, and how have those decisions affected the way you balance marriage and children?

Theme 1. I never thought not to work.

All participants had been working at least 10 years in their industry and were married or divorced. All but one had her own children; the exception was a woman who married a man with children. Participants said they were able to work and be married and have children. They did not think anything was unusual about it.

> I was working weekends and nights and traveling and pregnant. It never entered my mind that I would not work. I worked too hard to get to that point. . . . I won a top award while I was in the hospital having a baby. (Hunter)

> I was the only woman in the business. What is unique for me is I want to do things my way. It is difficult to shut work off. You just do it. I get up at 6:00 a.m. . . . and I make sure everyone at work and my children are doing what they have to do. It is not hard; it is about timing. You just do it, and it is part of my esteem. No way that I will not have a career. I never asked for anything, never for a promotion or a step up, just worked hard and this is what I do. I learned what I was good at, and that was what they hired me for; my uniqueness to get the job done. (Ruby)

If someone would have had a crystal ball and predicted that I would have the career I do, I would have never seen this as my future at all. . . . I worked harder not smarter. I could not turn down any assignment or any chance for promotion. . . . I love my child and believe every mother does, yet I am a single mom and I never took off early from work or missed an assignment. (Amber)

Be the best you can in the job you have, not the job you want to have. . . . I love what I do. I had to run a department, and it was a big stepping stone since I managed over 80 people in four locations and had to fire people, and I had both of my kids. My children see work comes first, yet I want them to know they come first. I started having breakfast with my children on Fridays until my son reached an age when he said sleep is more important than breakfast. (Megan)

In a male-dominated industry you are more like the men you work with than the women that do not work. . . . I have the presence because of the level I am at. I worked long hours: 12-14 hours days, nights, and weekends. . . . The value of relationships in business allows you to learn how to cope and deal with what needs to be handled, whether at work or at home, and knowledge and the opportunities grow. "Children are scary, give me a board room and I am fine. Give me a two-year-old and I will be on my knees, not knowing what to do. I will crumble. (Jasmine)

I was only paid if I did what I said I would do and I was producing. I was a control freak, and I loved to do what I did . . . and loved my family. (Kayla)

I was competitive and driven to do the absolute best at work and have a happy family. (Nora)

I never planned it…I thought I would be a teacher. I worked my way up. How to gain customers and build relationships is my strength. I am not looking for the next promotion; it just came up. (Sophie)

I was doing a good job at everything. Children make everything more complex. I just never thought not to work. (Violet)

Research Question 2

How have career choices been an opportunity (enhancement) or loss (conflict) regarding marriage and children?

Theme 2. Career is a positive influence on self.

The spillover theme emerged when participants said they assumed they could "do it all" and did not delayed getting married or having children. They described approaching work the same way they approached family and vice versa. Career was consistently rated as positive and an enhancement to their life. Participants rarely used the word *balance*; instead, they talked about prioritizing, multitasking, and adopting a "figure-it-out" attitude. They set priorities for both their home and work lives and expressed a desire to as successful in their parenting role as they were as professionals. They did acknowledge some guilt and concern that they were not always to be available for their children.

> I assumed I would be married and have children. I always worked and always took on a promotion . . . take on a department . . . never consider no. I can do this without a doubt, not a question or thought of anything else. I never said no and never left a meeting and never said I had to leave to get my child. (Amber)

> I always wanted to have a child. I tried with my first husband and it did not happen so at 36 I was pregnant and I was thrilled. I would take my baby with me in meetings on weekends. I was the top person and in charge, so I did not ask; I just did it. (Kayla)

> I never planned career, or children, never a question. I just thought I would figure it out. First kid, I was not a manager. With the second kid I was a manager and moved up to supervisor. I live in the moment and I do not think about the future. I cannot imagine not working. I just have to plan better, organize better, and qualify priorities at work and home better. (Megan)

Participants consistently rated their career as positive and an enhancement to their life. They used the following words to describe their career: self-esteem, identity, confidence, empowerment, purpose, prestige, first priority, critical. This study confirmed that women work because they are motivated by self-fulfillment and they love working, even if they want to have a family. None of the interviewees in the current study suggested that work interfered with their ability to pursue marriage and children. They enjoyed the corporate world and the challenge to move up the ladder and take on leadership responsibility. They acknowledge trade-offs but said they were worth making.

Theme 3. Career is a positive influence on marriage.

Participants believed their career affected their relationship with their husband positively. They said that family did not affect their satisfaction with work, but they also voiced a need to have supportive husbands.

> It would give him more opportunities and less stress to pursue his goals by having two incomes. My career was a benefit for my husband. He was not the only provider and we were allowed the opportunity to take risks. Both of us could since we had two incomes. (Sophie)

> I married at 23 and he was an underachiever. I was divorced and remarried to my [current] husband, who was the smartest man I know. I was a workaholic, and I married a man that was a workaholic. My husband married a woman that had a title, a powerful woman, and that is what I offered my husband. (Jasmine)

> Men are attracted to successful women. . . . I could not be home, and he understood I need to be happy, and he loves me. (Kayla)

> My husband tells me he loves me in spite of my job. He does not care where I work. For me the balance of power is important. It is more important to me for both of us to have an equal stake in the financial providing for the home. (Megan)

> Even when my husband was successful, I could not stay home; it was not my makeup. (Violet)

Theme 4. Career is a positive influence on children.

Participants believed their career contributed important benefits to their children, helping them develop independence, responsibility, and resilience. They described themselves as an anomaly compared to stay-at-home mothers or those working part-time. They dutifully worked family around their work schedule and described their choices as the best for their children. Most participants used hired help for child care (Figure 6).

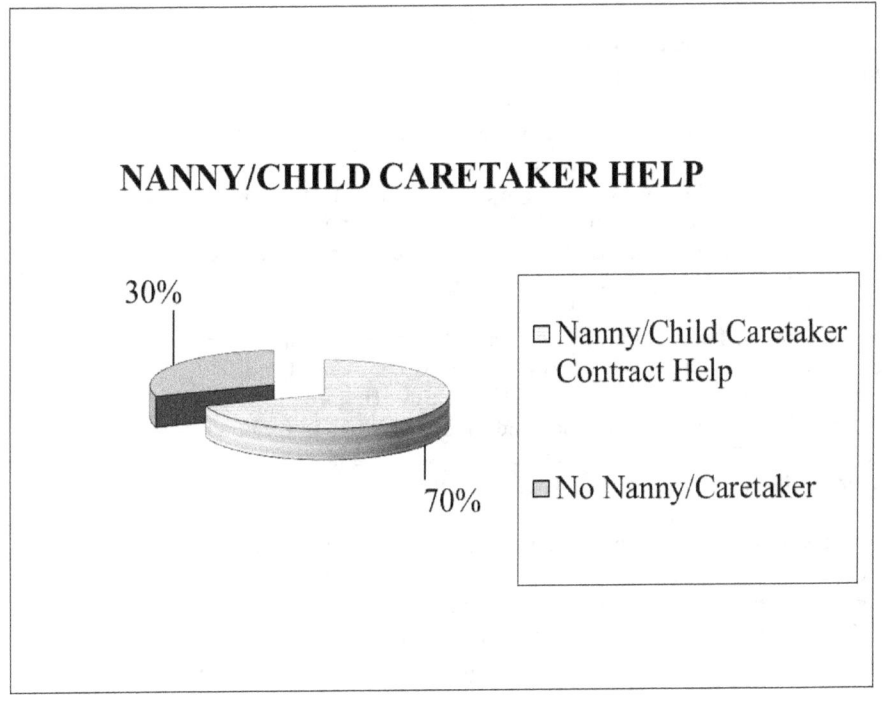

Figure 6. Paid child care assistance.

I had a nanny, and I had a boy and a girl. I worked up to the day I had my baby. There is a lot of challenges with kids, and I have grown more in that area. In a sales role I did not want to have kids. I was traveling and making lots of money. (Nora)

I had a nanny. I had someone to help out. I never wanted to leave my job, yet I thought I was selfish for my children. I went through five [nannies] before I contemplated not working. (Kayla)

My husband moved his office to home after five or six nannies and mental breakdown and stress. He said "I can take 20% less clients." Finding a caretaker you trust is the most important. (Megan)

Besides paid child care, participants also relied on neighboring stay-at-home

mothers to help them out if they were traveling or late from work. Some also relied on stay-at-home moms to keep them updated and remind them of school events. This was especially true for mothers of teenagers. In general, participants described the experience of being a working mother as a juggling act:

You have to make choices, and you have to decide what to do with the children. I would take a baby with me in meetings and on weekends. I was working and I was the top person. I did not ask; I just did it and I was in charge . . . . Work is easy; children are difficult. Younger is easier and teenager is more difficult. You just have to bake the cake and watch the temperature and make sure you do it all. (Kayla)

I got pregnant while I was working full time and working on my master's degree. I was on maternity leave and was breast feeding when I showed up to meet the head guy at a company I wanted to work for. He hired me. . . . Pregnancy was like every other project, and I handled it like every other project. Balance: When you have all those plates spinning and they do not crash. With more children you have more plates. (Violet)

Priority is being the best mother and the best at work as I could. Both are critical, and I was provider for my child so work was important or I could not support my child. My child is independent; he does not need me to cook. . . . A benefit to my son [is that he] was responsible, resilient. Through the years he makes it OK to consult me. He is ahead of the curve. (Amber)

Your kids are happy if you are happy. . . . When they are younger they are fine with someone to take care of them. They are in daycare and they need to be with other kids. It is a positive influence on the kids. One manager indicated that I would not come back after pregnancy, and I was so upset I wrote it down on a piece of paper and keep it because it made me angry that they would think it. I did get a manager's position, and then during that I had a second child and had men and one woman reporting to me. was so busy working that I pumped milk while I was in the car. I was in the van and I was breast feeding a child while my sales person was in with the account; otherwise, I would pump milk and put it in the refrigerator. (Hunter)

I made sure my daughter was taken care of so I could work long hours, travel. I could not take time off in my company if I wanted . . . to be taken seriously. We cannot appear to not be doing our jobs, and you would never ask to take time off. . . . All women have guilt with their children, yet there are positives for our children: independence, responsibility, and a positive role model. (Chloe)

Theme 5. Career responsibilities contribute to maternal guilt.

Although participants were generally positive about the effects of career on their children, they did admit to experiencing guilt as mothers. They considered guilt to be part of the package, something that all mothers feel. Executive women feel guilty when they fail to be home for dinner, forget an event, or have to scramble for creative ways to spend quality time with their children.

There is this feeling that if I had stayed at home with my son that he would have been different. My girl was fine; she is very strong and very driven. Yet there are stay-at-home moms where their children are in trouble. It happens. (Nora)

I remember when I had my luggage under my bed and was leaving for another trip, and my 18-month-old daughter sat on my luggage and said "no go," and that was it for me. . . . Questions you have: Now I have a child. Is this good for me? Is this good for the relationship? Do I want this? Yet I was being selfish. It was not supposed to be about me but about the child. Yet I cannot help but feel that I am not fulfilled with being a mom. . . . . I was out of the loop. I felt like a creep. All my friends bought [Christmas] gifts for the teachers except for me. [My son] did not say anything to me, yet I felt I should know that it is my responsibility. I decided we will give to teachers to buy New Years Eve bags to take. My comment to my son: "You will stand out and they received a million gifts from students, yet you are the only student to give gifts now." Now I have a child and do I want this, yet I was being selfish. It was not supposed to be about me but about the child. (Violet)

I think I am setting a good example for my children. They take it [my work] seriously. . . . They take responsibility for their actions and they see they need to be responsible and complete tasks. When they were younger they did not know: as long as they were taken care of. As they get older it is more difficult. I would get home at 6 or 7 p.m. and so our time was quality time: laundry, dishes done, so all of our time was playing and talking. We had time to do fun things, and I think that is what created our strong bond. Yes, sometimes my children were upset and cried and said the majority of moms at their school do not work. (Sophie)

I had a presentation on work-family balance, so I did some research and I explained the concept: 1-10, with 10 a 100%. I asked my older son what grade would you give me, and he said "I give you a 70." I said that is average, that is a C. What would make me get a 90 or 100? I was braced for the guilt trip. He said "Mom, you talk to me like I work for you, and if you did not use all those work words and you did not treat me like I work for you, then you would be a 90." Well that is not acceptable for a driven, type A personality, yet I said thank you for your feedback. He said "Mom, that is my point. You treat me like an employee and you just did. See, that is one of those words." My younger son said "I give you an 80," and I said "What can I do to get a 90?" He said "I would like you around." Children see work comes first, yet I want them to know they come first. I started having breakfast with my children on Fridays, until one day my son said sleep is more important than breakfast. I have good kids! (Megan)

As mothers we have guilt, and as the children get older it is more difficult to work because then they have activities after school and you cannot be there to help them. . . . [When they are] babies it is difficult for the woman, yet you do not think about it; you just do it. (Hunter)

Participants were unapologetic about wanting to work, and they described their relationships with their children positively. At the same time, they acknowledged feeling guilty at times that they were not able to be with their children as much as they would have liked. On the whole, they said their children benefited from having a working mother because it made them more independent and resilient.

Research Question 3

What sacrifices or regrets, if any, do you have?

Theme 6. I do not have regrets.

The women in this study acknowledged making some sacrifices to manage both career and a family, but they were reluctant to express any regrets. One sacrifice was the time to develop meaningful friendships with other women. Participants rarely used the word balance. Several brought it up because it is part of the title for this dissertation. But although they rarely used the word, balance was clearly important for them as they attempted to be employees, wives, and mothers.

Ruby used a creative metaphor to describe her attempt to find balance:
Cram the square peg into the round hole. Somehow we make if fit and it

becomes part of us and who we are. As women you can guide us, and then the problem is they [men] want to mold us into their mindset of doing things a certain way. Think it of a chest of drawers, and each drawer: career, personal, children . . . . We multitask, and men compartmentalize. Determine who you can live with and who you can live without, what you can live with and what you can live without.

The researcher posed a follow-up question: What advice would you give the next generation of younger women who are facing career decisions and balancing marriage and children?

I would not give advice to other women because they can do it all. They have choices, and they need to decide what they want to do. (Kayla)

Today hopefully women are at a place when they can have it all, they can balance by knowing who they are in the beginning. Hopefully, we paved the way for them so they are equal for the most part and now can have it all and balance work with marriage and children. (Jasmine)

Who am I to tell a younger woman she cannot reach her dreams and have a wonderful career, marriage, and children? (Amber)

I think the most important is you need a network of women that will give you support and give to you and you give to them. They are dream builders. (Violet)

For these executive women, their career is a major part of their identity. Having a career enhances confidence and self-esteem, qualities that help them deal with the challenges of maintaining their other roles as wives and mothers. But although they recognize these different roles, they see themselves as complete, unified persons: challenged, but not fractured, by the tasks of working and parenting.

Evidence of Quality

Evidence of quality in a study pertains to accuracy of data and confidence in the results. In assessing evidence of quality, typical components include member checks, an audit trail, and referential adequacy (Lincoln & Guba, 1985). This study employed a comparative analysis of three theoretical constructs (role theory, role conflict theory, and spillover theory) as they relate to career women, along with the researcher's experience as a career woman. This study also used member checking, whereby interviewees evaluate the accuracy and representativeness of their responses as transcribed or synthesized by a researcher (Moustakas, 1994). Member checking involved two executive women who were not interviewed. They were asked to comment on the relevance for their own lives of the themes identified in the study. In addition, participants were asked to review and confirm the accuracy of their interview transcripts. An audit trail was accomplished by maintaining electronic records of steps in data analysis and archiving audio recordings and the researcher's interview notes. Referential adequacy was achieved by identifying the data using the Stevick-Colizzi-Keen method to develop preliminary findings.

Summary

This chapter summarized the results of a qualitative study based on individual interviews with executive women. The phenomenological approach involved open-ended questions to engage participants in a conversation to describe their experience in pursuing a career while balancing the responsibilities of marriage and children. Results showed that for these women, identity and self-concept were fundamentally shaped by their careers. Although they acknowledged occasional guilt feelings about their inability to be fully present in their children's lives, they expressed no regrets about the decisions they made, and they described their children in positive, optimistic terms. Chapter 5 will analyze the study's results, draw conclusions from the data, and recommend areas for further research.

CHAPTER 5: SUMMARY, CONCLUSIONS, AND RECOMMENDATIONS

Introduction

The purpose of this qualitative study was to examine the viewpoints of executive women and the life choices they have made regarding career, marriage, and children. A phenomenological qualitative research design was used in order to elicit rich descriptions of the phenomenon. Results of individual interviews with participants revealed six major themes:

1. Participants never seriously entertained the idea of not working.

2. Participants said that career is a positive influence on self.

3. Participants said that career is a positive influence on marriage.

4. Participants said that career is a positive influence on children.

5. Participants said that career responsibilities contribute to maternal guilt.

6. While acknowledging having made sacrifices for their careers, participants did not express regrets.

Interpretation of Findings

This section is organized around the study's research questions and the themes that emerged in participants' responses. The first question asked "How have you made choices about career, and how have those decisions affected the way you balance marriage and children?" One theme emerged in response to this question: Participants never considered not working, and they expressed satisfaction in having successfully managed a career, marriage, and family. All of them moved up the ladder into supervisory and management positions while balancing family demands

The feminist movement provided equal educational opportunities for women, and by the 1990s women were prominent in the corporate world (Eagly, 1995; Jost & Kay,2005; Snyder, 2003). It took another generation, however, for women to achieve a substantial presence in executive positions. Participants in this study reflect a trend in the labor force at large: women achieving parity with men in receiving bachelor's degrees (Barnett, 2004, p. 159). All the participants had an undergraduate degree and three had a master's degree (see Figure 7).

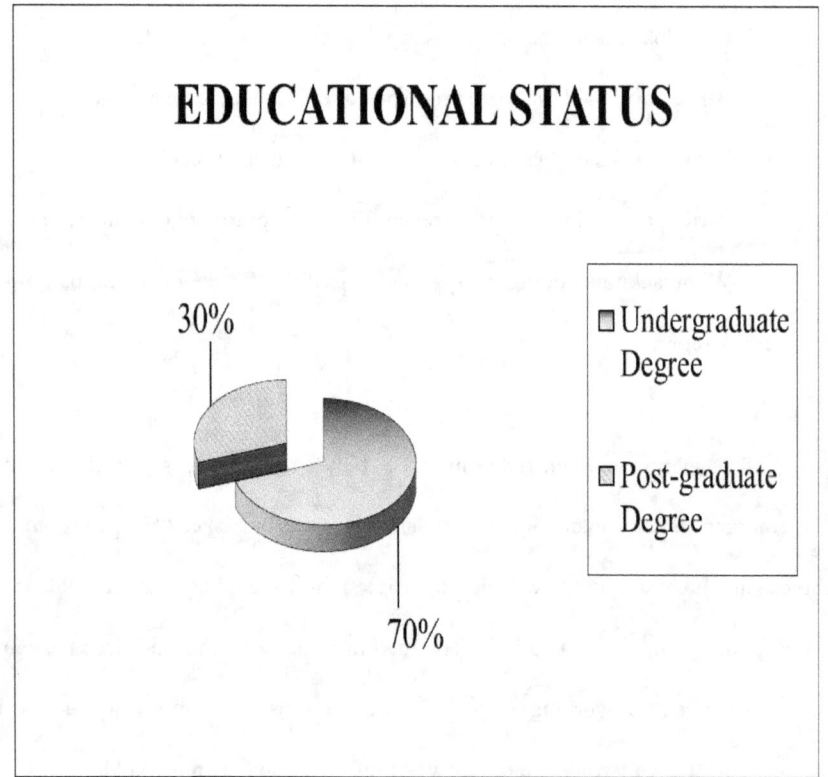

Figure 7. Educational status.

All participants were either married or divorced (see Figure 8). Half were currently married, and 30% had been divorced and then remarried. One urprising result was that these executive women had married comparatively early in life. In contrast to the national median age for marriage among women (26), 80% of participants in the current study married by age 23 (see Figure 3). In another respect, however, participants closely reflected national trends, in that several were single mothers for at least part of the time their children were growing up (see Figure 9).

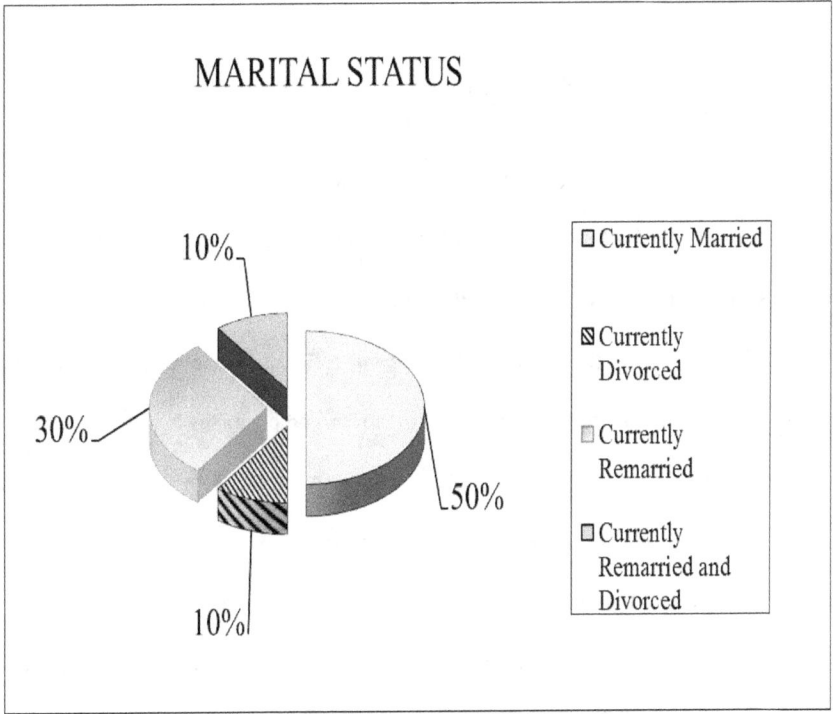

Figure 8. Marital status.

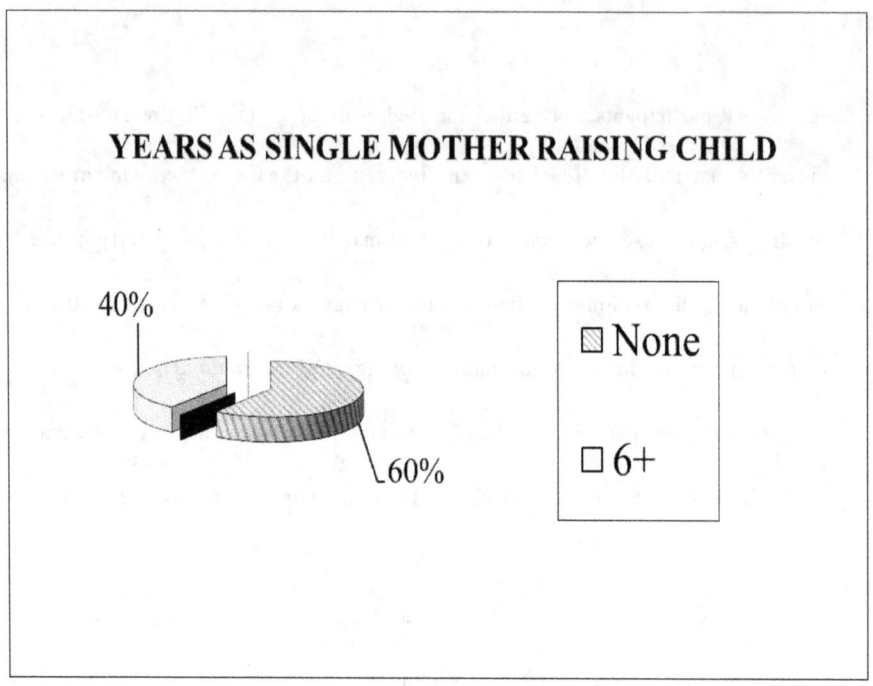

YEARS AS SINGLE MOTHER RAISING CHILD

40%

60%

None

6+

Figure 9. Number of years raising child(ren) as a single mother.

Other studies indicate that most career women delay marriage and children (Impett et al., 2005; Rothbard, 2001; Voydanoff & Donnelly, 1989) and that they expect to make difficult decisions about balancing career and family (Cinamon, 2006; Hakim, 2006). Participants in the present study did not reflect those trends. Nor did participants fit the generalization that entering the workforce compromises a woman's focus on family life (McElwain et al., 2005; Rothbard, 2001).

Greenhaus (2001) studied female accountants and found that "those that work to have a career will tolerate work interference to obtain the benefits of a high-level position" (p. 23). Participants in the current study did not convey the attitude that they had merely tolerated work interference; rather, they enjoyed work. They described their decision to pursue both family and career in matter-of-fact terms.

Prior to the 1970s, it was an anomaly for women to obtain advanced degrees and move up the executive ladder. It was not until the 1990s that large numbers of women had to balance work and marriage or family (Farber, 1996). None of the interviewees in the current study suggested that work interfered with their ability to pursue marriage and children. They enjoyed the corporate world and the challenge to move up the ladder and take on leadership responsibility. They acknowledge trade-offs but said they were worth making.

The second research question asked "How have career choices been an opportunity (enhancement) or loss (conflict) regarding marriage and children?" The wording of this question reflects the study's grounding in role theory, role conflict theory, and spillover theory. In role theory, women take on traditional domestic and child-rearing responsibilities. Role conflict theory assumes that one role (either work or family) will compromise the other, so work and family priorities are in conflict. In spillover theory, career and family can mutually enhance each other. One variation of spillover theory is the enhancement hypothesis, which suggests that for working women, positive attitudes enrich and negative attitudes deplete both work and family (Heller & Watson, 2005; Impett et al., 2005).

Several themes emerged in responses to this question. Participants described their careers as having a positive influence on themselves, on their marriages, and on their children. Despite an emphasis on how career choices enhanced their personal and family lives, participants did acknowledge conflict regarding maternal guilt. Hochschild (1997) concluded after a 3-year study that career women see work as an enhancement to their family life. Women who described themselves as working for a job had a higher incidence of role conflict than did career women. They may be motivated more by self-fulfillment and satisfaction than by financial exigency (Holahan & Gilbert, 1979). This study confirmed that women work because they are motivated by self-fulfillment and they love working, even if they want to have a family.

Participants in this study generally did not think that their career compromised their relationship with their husband. Indeed, several said their job enhanced their marriage. Regarding children, attitudes were mixed. Some women described the effects of their career on their children as positive spillover, whereas others acknowledged sometimes feeling guilty that their job compromised their role as mother. These women were already established in a career when they had children, and they tended to approach family life the same way they approached work: by being organized and persistent.

Maslow's (1999) theory of self-actualization is useful for understanding the attitudes of the women in this study.

> We learn about our own strengths and limits and extend them by overcoming difficulties, by straining ourselves to the utmost, by meeting challenge and hardship, even by failing. There can be great enjoyment in a great struggle and this can displace fear. Healthy self-esteem is based not only upon approval from others, but also upon actual achievements and successes and upon the realistic self-confidence which ensues. (p. 221)

Participants in this study were candid in describing the difficulties they had overcome, but they also affirmed Maslow's contention that struggle can yield enjoyment. These participants also illustrate the truth of the enhancement hypothesis, which suggests that for working women, positive attitudes enrich and negative attitudes deplete both work and family (Heller & Watson, 2005; Impett et al., 2005).

As was noted in chapter 2, few studies have addressed how husbands perceive a wife's career path. Greenhaus et al. (2001) found that improved family finances resulting from the wife working reduced some husband-wife conflict. Kossek and Ozeki (1998) found that people with high levels of conflict were less satisfied with their jobs and that family influence was unrelated to job satisfaction. In dual-career families, however, there were negative consequences of work-family conflict for women. Participants in the current study said that family did not affect their satisfaction with work, but they also voiced a need to have supportive husbands. Participants described their marriages in generally positive terms. Several paid tribute to supportive husbands, but they also acknowledge some parental inequality.

Research on women with careers suggests that they plan families later in life and have fewer children, compared to noncareer women (Cinanmon, 2006). Some studies have found that when women enter the work force, their ability to focus on family and home life is compromised (Jones et al., 2006; McElwain et al., 2005; Rothbard, 2001; Schneider & Waite, 2005). Most participants in the present study had their first child before age 30. One woman was unable to have children, but she helped raise three step-children. The majority of participants had two or three children.

Several studies have found that women struggle more than men do with guilt feelings regarding their family roles (Farber, 1996; Hochschild, 1997; Hyde et al., 1998). Participants in the current study admitted to feeling guilty that they did not spend enough time with their children. They found it difficult to avoid comparing themselves to stay-at-home mothers, whom they imagined being able to attend every school event and special occasion. Yet these women said the benefits of their career outweighed the detriments, and they did not regret their decisions. Several added that their children learned to be responsible and independent adults through the positive role of a working mother.

The third research question asked, "What sacrifices or regrets, if any, do you have?" In addition there was a follow-up question: "What advice would you give the next generation of younger women who are facing career decisions and balancing marriage and children?" Here the dominant theme was that although they acknowledged having made sacrifices for their careers, participants did not express any regrets. Advice to younger women is summed up by Amber's question: "Who am I to tell a younger woman they cannot reach their dreams and have a wonderful career, marriage and children?"

Tiedje et al. (1990) interviewed 200 professional women about their ability to balance career and family roles. The researchers found that participants did not perceive conflict and enhancement as opposite ends of the spectrum. The women in the current study revealed similar attitudes. Although they experienced some role conflict and acknowledged that their decision to have both a career and a family had resulted in sacrifices, they did not describe themselves as regretful. Regarding what advice they would offer the next generation, they displayed pride in their own accomplishments and optimism for the future.

Implications for Social Change

Social change is taking place, and as more women obtain higher education and pursue executive careers, there will be less stigma in the workplace as women work side by side with men or work with men as subordinates. Today, though, women in high-level executive positions still constitute a small minority. The results of this study can help women see that it is possible to pursue a demanding career and still have a meaningful marriage and family life. Women will see that having children and a career necessitates some sacrifices but that pursuing both can bring great fulfillment.

Recommendations for Further Action

This study and the results of the study impact gender regardless of race or sexual orientation. The liberation of women in general preceded the liberation or promotion of minority groups and those of a different sexual orientation. Therefore they got promoted during this time.

It is my opinion due to the political and social movements of minority groups I would expect to see women of great diversity being promoted in the next generation. I am gratified as we all should be to see that women since the liberation movement have made such progress within the corporate structure. The feminist movement paved the way for women in the 1970s, the mommy track in the 1990s, and women obtaining the education and experience in the 2000s to have an impact in leadership positions in corporate America.

This study was based on interviews with 10 executive women. As such, it represents their perceptions and attitudes at one moment in time. It would be interesting to follow a group of women over a period of time, perhaps checking in with them near the beginning of their careers, then again at midcareer, then again as they approach retirement to see how their perceptions change. Such a study would be quite ambitious, but any longitudinal study would yield a perspective that moment-in-time research cannot achieve.

Short of conducting a longitudinal study, researchers could compare the perceptions of women in MBA programs, who are still largely anticipating their careers, with experienced female executives. What do the younger women imagine it will be like to seek a position in the board room, and do they think they can do that and find space for the play room as well? How do their projections compare with those of seasoned career women?

Participants in this study see themselves as trailblazers. They recognize that the feminist movement created opportunities that their mothers did not have, and they are optimistic that their daughters will have even greater opportunities to make their way in what have historically been male-dominated industries. They see technological advancements as serving the interests of aspiring women, and they recognize that as women's numbers increase in upper management, so will their opportunities for female mentors and networks. These anticipated developments will provide the basis for much fruitful research.

Researcher's Experience

I had some preconceived ideas when I started this research that proved inaccurate. First, I thought women would say that at best one can hope to accomplish only two of three desires: career, marriage, and children. Instead, the women I interviewed affirmed that it is possible to have all three. They were mostly content to hire others to do housework and some child care, leaving them to concentrate on their jobs and on spending quality time with their children. I was surprised at how committed these women were to motherhood and to being involved in their children's lives. Second, I thought that the higher a woman moved in her career, the more difficult it would be to balance that part of her life with family. Instead, my interviewees said that they worked more hours earlier in their career in an effort to move up. Several spoke about the advantage of being the boss and deciding if and when to bring a child to work. And third, I expected to encounter more women who waited to have children until they were near 40, but these executives had theirs when they were in their 20s and early 30s.

The effects of the interviews on me were both pride and amazement at the life stories that were shared. Particularly significant, was how driven these women were to accomplish so much in their life and how they could reach the extraordinary heights in their professional careers while still balance marriage, and children. Not having shared their rise to these higher executive levels, allowed me to stay objective and maintain perspective. My preconceived notions regarding the inability of top executive women to successfully balance career, marriage, and children has changed.

These women demonstrated that other women entering executive career paths can be successful, happy and "have it all"; career, marriage, and children. My goal is to continue to focus on research after my Ph.D. to obtain more insight into this group of executive women, to open doors for other women in the midst of their struggles of how to juggle career with a family, and to provide valuable information and encouragement to women deciding whether to enter into and pursue an executive career path.

Summary

Today, women have opportunities and choices that were unheard of a generation ago. They are obtaining advanced degrees, and corporate American is increasingl willing to hire and promote them. More and more of them are driven, responsible, confident, and determined to succeed in business.

This phenomenological research found that executive women who were studied are proud of their accomplishments and firm in their conviction that combining career, marriage, and family was the right thing to do. They believe that their job and their family life have influenced each other positively, yet they have not entirely escaped the guilt that attends traditional expectations of the maternal role. Both role conflict theory and spillover theory, then, are useful in explaining their personal and professional lives.

These executive women still live in what is mostly a man's world, but they have carved out a place for themselves there. The particular challenge they have faced in that effort is well illustrated by a comment from Amber:

> I would go in my office when I was upset at work, close the door and lean over my desk and let the tears drop on the desk so they would not touch my face and ruin my mascara. We as women learn to get things done. We want to be strong, and if we cry we do it in private.

The experiences of these women who formed the basis of this study suggest that career, marriage, and children are not three separate roads. Instead, they are like three streams that unite to form a great river.

REFERENCES

Abele, A. E. (2003). The dynamics of masculine-agentic and feminine-communal traits: Findings from a prospective study. *Journal of Personality and Social Psychology, 85,* 775-776.

Adams, G. A., King, L. A., & King, D. W. (1996). Relationships of job and family involvement, family social support and work-family conflict with job and life satisfaction. *Journal of Applied Psychology, 81,* 411-420.

Archer, J. (1996). Sex differences in social behavior: Are the social role and evolutionary explanations compatible? *American Psychologist, 51,* 909-917.

Bandura, A., & Locke, E. A. (2003). Negative self-efficacy and goal effects revisited. *Journal of Applied Psychology, 88,* 87-99.

Bandura, A., & Jourden, F. J. (1991). Self-regulatory mechanisms governing the impact of social comparison on complex decision making. *Journal of Personality and Social Psychology, 60,* 941-951.

Barnett, R. C. (2004). *Women and multiple roles: Myths and reality.* Waltham, MA: Brandeis University, Women's Studies Research Center.

Basgall, J., & Snyder C. R. (1988). Excuses in waiting: External locus of control and reactions to success-failure feedback. *Journal of Personality and Social Psychology 54,* 656-662.

Baumeister, R. F. (2000). Gender differences in erotic plasticity: The female sex drive as socially flexible and responsive. *Psychological Bulletin, 126,* 347-374.

Berdahl, J. L., & Anderson, C. (2005). Men, women and leadership centralization in groups over time. *Group Dynamics Theory, Research, and Practice, 9,* 45-57.

Buffardi, L. C., Smith, J. L., O'Brien, A. S., & Erdwins, C. J. (1999). The impact of dependent-care responsibility and gender on work attitudes. *Journal of Occupational Health Psychology, 4,* 356-367.

Burke, R. J. (2004). Work and personal life integration. *International Journal of Stress Management, 11,* 299-304.

Caprara, G. V., Regalia, C., Scabini, E., Barbaranelli, C., & Bandura, A. (2004). Assessment of filial, parental, marital, and collective family beliefs. *European Journal of Psychological Assessment, 20,* 247-261.

Cardenas, R. A., Major, D. A., & Bernas, K. H. (2004). Exploring work and family distractions: Antecedents and outcomes. *International Journal of Stress Management, 11,* 346-365.

Cinamon, R. G., (2006). Anticipated work-family conflict: Effects of gender, self-efficacy, and family background. *Career Development Quarterly, 54,* 202-215.

Collier, P. J., & Callero, P. J. (2005). Role theory and social cognition: Learning to think like a recycler. *Self and Identity, 4,* 45-85.

Creswell, J. W. (2007). *Qualitative inquiry and research design: Choosing among five traditions* (2nd ed.). Thousand Oaks, CA: Sage.

Davis, P. G., Spencer, S. J., & Steele, C. M. (2005). Clearing the air: Identity safety moderates the effects of stereotype threat on women's leadership aspirations. *Journal of Personality and Social Psychology, 88,* 276-287.

Edwards, V. J., & Spence, J. T. (1987). Gender-related traits, stereotypes, and schemata. *Journal of Personality and Social Psychology, 53,* 146-154.

Eagly, A. H. (1995). The science and politics of comparing women and men. *American Psychologist, 50,* 145-158.

Farber, R. S. (1996). An integrated perspective on women's career development within a family. *The American Journal of Family Therapy, 24,* 329-342.

Friedman, S. D., & Greenhaus, J. H. (2000). *Work and family: Allies or enemies? What happens when business professionals confront life choices?* Oxford, NY: Oxford University Press.

Frone, M. R., Russell, M., & Cooper, M. L. (1992). Antecedents and outcomes of work-family conflict: Testing a model of work-family interface. *Journal of Applied Psychology, 77,* 65-78.

Goren, E. (2003). America's love affair with technology: The transformation of sexuality and the self over the 20th century. *Psychoanalytic Psychology, 20,* 487-508.

Grandey, A. A., Cordeiro, B. L., & Crouter, A. C. (2005). A longitudinal and multi-source test of the work-family conflict and job satisfaction relationship. *Journal of Occupational and Organizational Psychology, 78,* 305-323.

Graves, L. M., Ohlott, P. J., & Ruderman, M. N. (2007). Commitment to family roles: Effects on managers' attitudes and performance. *Journal of Applied Psychology, 92,* 44-56.

Greenhaus, J. H., & Beutell, N. J. (1985). Sources of conflict between work and family roles. *Academy of Management Review 10,* 76-88.

Greenhaus, J. H., & Parasuraman, S. (1986). A work-nonwork interactive perspective of stress and its consequences. *Journal of Organizational Behavior Management, 8,* 37-60.

Greenhaus, J. H., Parasuraman, S., & Collins, K. M. (2001). Career involvement and family involvement as moderators of relationships between work-family conflict and withdrawal from a profession. *Journal of Occupational Health Psychology, 6,* 91-100.

Hakim, C. (2006). Women, careers and work-life preferences. *British Journal of Guidance & Counseling, 34,* 279-292.

Hammack, P. L. (2005). Advancing the revolution in the science of sexual identity development. *Human Development, 48,* 303-308.

Hammer, L. B., Cullen, J. C., Neal, M .B., Sinclair, R. R., & Shafiro, M.V. (2005). The longitudinal effects of work-family conflict and positive spillover in depressive symptoms among dual-earner couples. *Journal of Occupational Health Psychology, 10,* 138-154.

Hanson, G. C., Hammer, L. B., & Colton, C. L. (2006). Development and validation of a multidimensional scale of perceived work-family positive spillover. *Journal of Occupational Health Psychology, 11,* 249-265.

Haverkamp, B. E., Morrow, S. L., & Ponterotto, J. G. (2005). A time and place for qualitative and mixed methods in counseling psychology research. *Journal of Counseling Psychology, 52,* 123-125.

Heilman, M. E., Wallen, A. S., Fuchs, D., & Tamkins, M. M. (2004). Penalties for success: Reactions to women who succeed at male gender-typed tasks. *Journal of Applied Psychology, 89,* 416-427.

Heller, D., & Watson, D. (2005). The dynamic spillover of satisfaction between work and marriage: The role of time and mood. *Journal of Applied Psychology, 90,* 1273-1279.

Hewlett, S. A. (2002). Executive women and the myth of having it all. *Harvard Business Review, 4,* 66-73.

Hewlett, S. A., & Luce, C .B. (2006). Opting out or opting in? *Global Agenda, 4,* 156-158.

Hewlett, S. A., & Luce, C. B. (2005). Off-ramps and on-ramps: Keeping talented women on the road to success. *Harvard Business Review, 3,* 43-54.

Higgins, C., Duxbury, L., & Lee, C. (2001). Impact of life-cycle stage and gender on the ability to balance work and family responsibilities. *Family Relations, 43,* 144-150.

Hochschild, A. (1997). *The time bind.* New York: Viking Publishing.

Holahan, C. K., & Gilbert, L. A. (1979). Interrole conflict for working women: Careers versus jobs. *Journal of Applied Psychology, 64,* 56-90.

Hook, M. K., Gerstein, L. H., Detterich, L., & Gridley, B. (2003). How close are we? Measuring intimacy and examining gender differences. *Journal of Counseling and Development, 81,* 461-472.

Hyde, J. S. (2005). The gender similarities hypothesis. *American Psychologist, 60,* 581-592.

Hyde, J. S., DeLamater, J. D., & Durik, A. M. (2001). Sexuality and the dual-earner couple, part II: Beyond the baby years. *Journal of Sex Research, 39,* 10-23.

Hyde, J. S., DeLamater, J. D., & Hewitt, E. C. (1998). Sexuality and the dual-earner couple: Multiple roles and sexual functioning. *Journal of Family Psychology, 12,* 354-368.

Impett, E. A., Gable, S. L., & Peplau, L. A. (2005). Giving up and giving in: The costs and benefits of daily sacrifice in intimate relationships. *Journal of Personality and Social Psychology, 89,* 327-344.

Jackson, A. P., & Scharman, J. S. (2002). Constructing family-friendly careers: Mothers' experiences. *Journal of Counseling & Development, 80,* 180-187.

Johnson, D. R., & Wu, J. (2002). An empirical test of crisis, social selection, and role explanations of the relationship between marital disruption and psychological distress: A pooled time-series analysis of four-wave panel data. *Journal of Marriage and Family, 64,* 211-224.

Johnson-Bailey, J., & Tisdell, E. J. (1998). Diversity issues in women's career development. *New Directions for Adult and Continuing Education, 80,* 83-93.

Johnston, M. (2007). Billionaire women we envy. *Forbes.* Retrieved June 24, 2007, from http://www.forbes.com http://www.forbes.com/2007/03/06/women-rich-envy-cz_mj_0306women.html

Jones, C. M., Braithwaite, V. A., & Healy, S. D. (2003). The evolution of sex differences in spatial ability. *Behavioral Neuroscience, 17,* 403-411.

Jones, F., Burke, R., & Westman, M. (Eds.). (2006). *Work-life balance: A psychological perspective.* New York: Psychological Press.

Josselson, R. (1987). *Finding herself.* San Francisco: Jossey-Bass.

Jost, J. T., & Kay, A. C. (2005). Exposure to benevolent sexism and complementary gender stereotypes: Consequences for specific and diffuse forms of system justification. *Journal of Personality and Social Psychology, 88,* 498-509.

Kiecolt, K. J. (2003). Satisfaction with work and family life: No evidence of a cultural reversal. *Journal of Marriage and Family, 65,* 23-35.

Kiecolt-Glaser, J. K., & Newton, T. L. (2001). Marriage and health: His and hers. *Psychology Bulletin, 127,* 472-503.

Kirchmeyer, C. (2002). Change and stability in managers' gender roles. *Journal of Applied Psychology, 87,* 929-939.

Kossek, E. E., & Ozeki, C. (1998). Work-family conflict, policies and the job-life satisfaction relationship: A review and directions for organizational behavior-human resources research. *Journal of Applied Psychology 83,* 139-149.

Kroll, L., & Faas, A. (Eds.) (2007). The world's richest people. *Forbes.* Retrieved June 17, 2007, from http://www.forbes.com 2007/03/06/billionaires-new-richest.

Lincoln, Y. S., & Guba, E. G. (1985). *Naturalistic inquiry.* Thousand Oaks: CA, Sage.

Livingston, M. M., Burley, K., & Springer, T. P. (1996). The importance of being feminine: Gender, sex role, occupational and marital role commitment and their relationship to anticipated work-family conflict. *Handbook of Gender Research, 5,* 179-192.

Lucas, M. (1997). Identity development, career development, and psychological separation from parents: Similarities and differences between men and women *Journal of Counseling Psychology, 44,* 123-132.

Lyness, K. S., & Judiesch, M. K. (2001). Are female managers quitters? The relationships to gender, promotions, and family leaves of absence to voluntary turnover. *Journal of Applied Psychology, 86,* 1167-1178.

Lyness, K. S., & Thompson, D .E. (1997). About the glass ceiling: A comparison of matched samples of female and male executives. *Journal of Applied Psychology, 82,* 359-375.

Lyness, K. S., & Thompson, D. E. (2002). Climbing the corporate ladder: Do female and male executives follow the same route? *Journal of Applied Psychology, 85,* 86.

Lyubomirsky, S., King, L., & Diener, E. (2005). The benefits of frequent positive affect: Does happiness lead to success? *Psychological Bulletin, 131,* 803-855.

Marks, S. P. (1977). Multiple roles and role strain: Some notes on human energy, time and commitment. *American Sociological Review, 42,* 921-936.

Marks, G., & Houston, D. M. (2002). The determinants of young women's intentions about education, career development and family life. *Journal of Education and Work, 15,* 321-336.

Maroda, K. J. (2004). A relational perspective on women and power. *Psychoanalytic Psychology, 21,* 428-435.

Maslow, A. H. (1999). *Toward a psychology of being* (3rd ed.). New York: Wiley.

McBride, A. B. (1990). Mental health effects of women's multiple roles. *American Psychologist, 45,* 381-384.

McCracken, R. S., & Weitzman, L. M. (1997). Relationship of personal agency, problem-solving appraisal, and traditionality of career choice to women's attitudes toward multiple role planning. *Journal of Counseling Psychology, 2,* 149-159.

McEvan, B. S. (2005). Stressed or stressed out: What is the difference? *Journal of Psychiatry Neuroscience, 30,* 315-318.

McElwain, A. K., Korabik, K., & Rosin, H. M. (2005). An examination of gender differences in work-family conflict. *Behavioral Science, 37,* 35-52.

Mennino, S. F., Rubin, B. A., & Brayfield, A. (2005). Home-to-job and job-to-home spillover: The impact of company policies and workplace culture. *Sociological Quarterly, 46,* 107-135.

Miller, G. E., Cohen, S., & Ritchey, A. K. (2002). Chronic psychological stress and the regulation of pro-inflammatory cytokines: A gucocorticoid-resistance model. *Health Psychology, 21,* 531-541.

Moustakas, C. (1994). *Phenomenological research methods.* Thousand Oaks, CA: Sage.

Nastasi, B. K., & Schensul, S. L. (2005). Contributions of qualitative research to the validity of intervention research. *Journal of School Psychology, 43,* 177-195.

Netemeyer, R. G., Boles, J. S., & McMurrian, R. (1996). Development and validation of work-family conflict and family-work conflict scales. *Journal of Applied Psychology, 81,* 400-410.

Parasuraman, S., & Greenhaus J. H. (Eds.). (1999). *Integrating work and family: Challenges and choices for a changing world.* Westport, CT: Praeger Publishers.

Perrone, K. M., Civiletto, C. L., Webb, L. K., & Fitch, J. (2004). Perceived barriers to and supports of attainment of career and family goals among academically talented individuals. *International Journal of Stress Management, 11,* 114-131.

Perrone, K. M., & Worthington Jr., E. L. (2001). Factors influencing ratings of martial quality by individuals within dual-career marriages: A conceptual model. *Journal of Counseling Psychology, 48,* 3-9.

Perry-Jenkins, M., Repetti, R. L., & Crouter, A. C. (2000). Work and family in the 1990s. *Journal of Marriage and the Family, 62,* 981-998.

Ragins, B. R., & Cotton, J. L. (1999). Mentor functions and outcomes: A comparison of men and women in formal and informal mentoring relationships. *Journal of Applied Psychology, 84,* 529-550.

Rosenfeld, H. W. (1964). Social choice conceived as a level of aspiration. *Journal of Abnormal and Social Psychology, 68,* 491-499.

Rothbard, N. P. (2001). Enriching or depleting? The dynamics of engagement in work and family roles. *Administrative Science Quarterly, 46,* 655-684.

Schensul, J. J., & LeComopte, M. D. (Eds.). (1999). *Ethnographer's toolkit: Volumes 1-7.* Walnut Creek, CA: AltaMira Press.

Schneider, B., & Waite, L. J. (Eds.). (2005). *Being together working apart: Dual-career families and the work-life balance.* New York: Cambridge University Press.

Simpson, P. A., & Stroh, L. K. (2004). Gender differences: Emotional expression and feelings of personal inauthenticity. *Journal of Applied Psychology, 89,* 715-721.

Snyder, M. (2003). Women determine development: The unfinished revolution. *Journal of Women in Culture and Society, 29,* 223-225.

Spitze, G. (1988). Women's employment and family relations: A review. *Journal of Marriage and the Family, 50,* 595-618.

Steenbergen, E. F., Ellemers, N., & Mooijaart, A. (2007). How work and family can facilitate each other: Distinct types of work-family facilitation and outcomes for women and men. *Journal of Occupational Health Psychology, 12,* 279-300.

Strauss, A., & Corbin, J. (1990). *Basics of qualitative research: Grounded theory procedures and techniques.* Thousand Oaks, CA: Sage.

Teasdale, J. D., Moore, F., Scott, J., & Pope, M. (2001). How does cognitive therapy prevent relapse residual depression? Evidence from a controlled trial. *Journal of Consulting and Clinical Psychology, 69,* 347-357

Tiedje, L. B., Wortman, C. B., Downey, G., Emmons, C., Biernat, M., & Lang, L. (1990). Women with multiple roles: Role-compatibility perceptions, satisfaction, and mental health. *Journal of Marriage and the Family, 52,* 63-72.

Tinklin, T., Croxford, L., Ducklin, A., & Frame, B. (2005). Gender and attitudes to work and family roles: The views of young people at the millennium. *Gender and Education, 17,* 129-142.

Van Lange, P. A. M., Drigotas, S. M., Rusbult, C. E., Arriaga, X. B., Witcher, B. S., & Cox, C.L. (1997). Willingness to sacrifice in close relationship. *Journal of Personality and Social Psychology 72,* 1373-1395.

Voydanoff, P., & Donnelly, B. W. (1989). Work and family roles and psychological distress. *Journal of Marriage and the Family, 51,* 923-932.

Waner, K. K., Winter, J. K., & Breshears, R. G. (2005). Family issues in the workplace: Are students on track? *Journal of Education for Business, 1,* 145-148.

Wentling, R. M. (1998). Work and family issues: Their impact on women's career development. *New Directions for Adult and Continuing Education, 80,* 15-24.

Wertz, F. J. (2005). Phenomenological research methods for counseling psychology. *Journal of Counseling Psychology, 52,* 167-177.

Wolcott, H. F. (1990). *Writing up qualitative research.* Thousand Oaks, CA: Sage.

Wong, K. F. E., Yik, M., & Kwong, J. Y. Y. (2006). Understanding the emotional aspects of escalation of commitment: The role of negative affect. *Journal of Applied Psychology, 91,* 282-297.

Zhao, H., Seibert, S. E., & Hills, G. E. (2003). The mediating role of self-efficacy in the development of entrepreneurial intentions. *Journal of Applied Psychology, 90,* 1265-1272.

Format is based on NVivo8 software.
Goal is to develop common themes.

Brief background is given for each participant. This is followed by common themes by participant. All uses of "I" and "my" are quotations from participant interviews.

Participant: Amber

Background Information

VP, married, divorced with one child. She was married in her 20s. She had a strong mother who worked and raised 7 girls as well as was married. She indicated she did not see her parents as having a good marriage. Her mom taught the daughters to take care of and provide for themselves. There was never a question about college or working. She started working at age 16 and always worked. She indicates she moved in a neighborhood where most the mothers at her sons' school did not work. So she depended on them to pick up her son or take care of him when she h ad to travel or work late. They were her support system since no family in the city. She felt they thought she was different yet she was the only one that was a single mom so the other mothers had a husband, children and stayed home to take care of domestic. As a result, she could depend on them at a moment's notice to take her child.

How have you made choices about career and how did those decisions affect the way you balance marriage and children?

Career Choices/Decisions

I never thought not to work.
The expectation was that I would attend college and work. I worked to pay my way through college. I always had a job; waitress, cleaned apartments.
My industry started out as all women and then when I moved into management it was a combination of men and women.
Career is a benefit.
Career is just what I do, I love what I do. I love my work.
I never thought about balance. I just took on additional roles and never turned down a promotion or an opportunity to take on more assignments and responsibility.
I enjoy my work.
It is my passion and what I do.

Career Path

Always knew I would work. Worked on my Masters while I was working so in some way did want to move up in a position. Did not expect to move to the level I am at now.
I never planned to be in management.
I was good at what I did and I was promoted for my abilities. There was no training, no concept of what makes a manager I just learned and was good at it.
I can do it all without a doubt no question or thoughts of anything else.
Always work and always take a promotion.
I never said no and never left a meeting. Never would say I had to pick up my child. I just made it work.
I would take on another department and never considered to say no.
I worked harder than the men. Not smarter than the men yet in our generation we worked and did anything that was asked of us.
Just did it took on promotions and I did not need to talk to my husband
I can do it all.
My identity is my career
It is important to have accomplishments and career allows that to happen.
Loyalty is most important more than pay.

Work Traits

Women handle situations differently and as you move up you take on traits to be strong.
Worked hard
Good at what I did
Reliable
Strong
Confident

Career Effect on Family

I just waiting until I met the man I thought I would be with forever because that is what my parents did. I planned to be married and have children. After we were married for a few years I planned to have a baby. I knew I wanted to get married and waited until I was in my 20s because I wanted to make marriage forever, I always knew I would have a child. I planned that is what you did. I never thought about it. I never thought not to work. My husband I just worked and I was attending school for my Masters and then we decided to have a child. I never thought not to work even when I had the baby. I was working full time, pregnant and never thought about it as unusual. I assumed I could handle work, baby and domestic tasks. I was pregnant had the child and was back at work.

Mentors and Advisors

My mom was my role model.

My supervisors and bosses were my mentors and the ones that were my mentors were women

They would have me promoted when they were promoted.

They would answer questions and help me in management situations.

<u>Support System</u>

My support system was stay at home moms. They would pick up my child and take care of him when I was traveling or had to stay late at a meeting. I had a great support group of stay at home moms that were in the suburb area where we live.

How have career choices been an opportunity (enhancement) or conflict (loss) regarding marriage and children?

<u>Positive Spillover to Self</u>

Career was a benefit.

Career was security.

Career defines my life.

Career gives you the opportunity to make decisions. You can decide what you want.

Career is about financial stability - buy the house and the car.

Focus on being the best – the best mother, the best employee.

<u>Positive Spillover to Marriage</u>

Yes, we both were working and could have a nice house and provide. When we had a child it changed our marriage to the negative. Yet, it allowed me to make a decision to divorce my husband. My roles were changing yet I did not see my husband role changing. She did take on the additional roles of picking up dry cleaning, cooking, shopping and domestic tasks.

Felt her husband did not change when they had a child. It was easier to work and take care of child then to be married. She indicated he did not change his life and would see his friends, go hunting do other activities yet she had no break. There was not an equal sharing in the raising of their child. So instead of making them closer it made them farther apart.

<u>Positive Spillover to Children</u>

Yes, it taught him responsibility.

He learned to be resilient through the years. He makes it OK to consult me.

He is ahead of the curb and has learned much by seeing me work hard.

He knew I was the provider and my work provided for my child. He learned to be independent. Now he is independent and does not need me to cook, he can get his own meal and it is lonelier.

Before I enjoy being the best mom and the best employee and felt she did a great job at both.

Negative: Conflict to Self

I left out me, doing things for myself.

Negative: Conflict to Marriage

I was picking up more and yet he was hiring help for the lawn and he made sure he was out with his friends and I felt like I was taking on more responsibility. His answer was to have another child and I knew that I could not do it all without his being an overachiever like me. Career was my enjoyment. It was easier on my own. My husband was shocked by this attitude and never thought I would walk away from the huge house and perfect neighborhood. Yet, his negativity and underachiever was more work. It was better for my child to be in a less stressful situation so he would not see the discord of my marriage. I decided that the husband was more of a burden then being a single mom and taking care of my child. It was more work than it was worth in the marriage. Easier to divorce because I could take care of myself and my son and had one less difficult situation when the marriage was not working. The money and big house did not mean as much to me because I could provide and I had options.

Negative: Conflict to Children

As a mother there is always guilt that I missed an event, I had to work late and I could not be there.

What sacrifices if any did you make in pursuing a career? What regrets if any do you have?

Sacrifices to Self

Yes, in some ways just too busy to spend linger time for me. I would like to meet a man that is a partner. He needs to be successful and someone I can share my life with. As my child is older he does not need me as much so being with someone would be nice.

Sacrifices to Family

No86
Regrets

No

Advice to Younger Women

No advice – they should do it all. Maybe they can do it all and have the perfect marriage that would complement children. Career, marriage and a child were all a choice for me. I believe all girls should have the dream that she did that you can "have it all" in your life. It is important to have a supportive husband. I am unsure where the problems with my ex husband occurred. He was shocked when I asked for a divorce. It was just easier without a husband because there was not that support or what was needed to keep the relationship.

Participant: Chloe

Background

Meeting planner and had a lot of different jobs first significant one was started out for the Starwood Hotel business. I love the hotel, hospitality business. She moved up in that hotel from sales manager to assistant director sales and then national director of sales. She had from 10 to 40 people reporting to me both men and women. She was director of national sales office for 6 states and then due to downsizing and became director of corporate training.

How have you made choices about career and how did those decisions affect the way you balance marriage and children?

Career Choices/Decisions

At the beginning of my career I did not have a choice because my husband and I wanted both incomes. After I was divorced I was a single mom and so of course I worked.
I had a lot of different jobs the first significant one was in the Hotel business. I love the hotel, hospitality business. I moved up in that hotel from sales manager to assistant director sales and then national director of sales. I had from 10 to 40 people reporting to me both men and women. I was director of national sales office for 6 states and then due to downsizing and I became director of corporate training. Then I did marketing and leader for marketing.

Career Path

Always worked and never thought about it. 87
Never thought not to work
Loved working and loved the opportunity
Enjoyed my work
Moved up the ladder to management
I just was lucky because I was with a great company and continued to get promoted.
Traveled a lot and worked a lot of hours

Never turned down a promotion. I turned down a chance to move to NYC and stopped moving up after that.
Lucked into a great career
I could not take any time off in my company if I wanted to I had as a woman we had to work harder to be taken serious
Never ask to take time off the company for your family because you will not move up the ladder
Actually once I was established then I could work more flexible hours. With moving up the ladder and creditability it allows more flexibility because the company wants you to stay and knows your abilities

Work Traits

Aggressive
Work harder not smarter
Ask for what you want
People person
Take on challenges
Be visible in your company

Career Effect on Family

After divorce it was 14 years before I married again so I was a single mom and a career woman and waiting for the right guy. When you have children you need the right guy that will gel with them and it just took awhile.
I could take care of myself and being busy with a child does change your time priorities. When you can take care of yourself and your child you want to meet the right man or otherwise go it alone.
People ask how do you do it and you do not think about it you just do it.
There is not a reflection of how to accomplish it you just must get it done.

Mentors and Advisors

Mentor – guy who hired me and another woman that is VP at Starwood and always worked in the industry and she has always given good advice. She was in a different department than me and we always talked and she helped me in making decisions and influencing ideas. 88

Support System

The woman I was around was all related to business. I did not interface with stay at home moms. Most of the women were staying at home moms so I was different for them. I was more comfortable with men and women that worked. I did not have many stay at home mom friends.

How has career choices been an opportunity (enhancement) or conflict (loss) regarding marriage and children?

Positive Spillover to Self

Career was positive for me personally; it was a wonderful great time and it was who I was and what I do. I made time for my girlfriends most were in the industry or working women. Looking back I think I was too much concentrated on my career and not enough on developing friends in town. My friends were all in the business and out of town so I wish I had developed more personal friendships than business friendships. I was with the business associates all day and I was with them and then when not I was at home.

Positive Spillover to Marriage

First husband I married and was young and we grew apart. It was not career I was still working to move into a career. My ex husband was supportive to help with child even after the divorce.

Second husband who I am with now was supportive. Yet, I married him in my late 30s. My husband was not going to move out of Texas and take a job out of state. Anywhere in state was fine. The business I was in I was with the clients and I had a husband that was very social and easy to work with since he had no children. He was always supportive of me and an asset to my social events at work.

Positive Spillover to Children

I made sure my daughter was taken care of so I could work long hours; travel.
I never had to take on the domestic activities; cooking and cleaning. I feel like I am a nurturer. My daughter did go to daycare and my ex husband would take care of her. So I had my career and I planned to travel and handled someone to take care of her. Most women at that time were stay at home moms. I had different life as a single mom than when someone is married. You lose friends when you divorce.

Negative: Conflict to Self

Maybe did not develop the range of girl friends that I could have since I was focused on work. 89
Negative: Conflict to Children

Some guilt with children – yet believe all women have some guilt with their children and women stated positives to their children; independence, responsibility and positive role model.
Ask her, my daughter is a stay at home mom. I thought she would take after me and have a career.

What sacrifices if any did you make in pursuing a career? What regrets if any do you have?

<u>Sacrifices to Self</u>

When I was single mom but the company knew and so I they did not offer new positions to move – yet I stilled moved up the ladder yet I do believe if I would have been more open to take positions I would have moved up faster and into better positions so it was a sacrifice for my career. I could have moved up farther if I would have been willing to move to different cities more often.

<u>Sacrifices to Family</u>

Regret only for my child that I was not there enough for her or I missed events. And my daughter says "oh mom you had to do what you had to do".

<u>Regrets</u>

No

<u>Advice to Younger Women</u>

None, hopefully they can do it all. Work has changed drastically now; I believe companies are more accommodating to women and their children. If I wanted to go to a program and I could not and I never did and I never left the office I work long hard hours. Today I believe that the women can leave and go back later and do not have to work the hours we do as we were leaders in the field.

Hunter

<u>Background</u>

She has a college degree in communications. She graduated and move to Dallas to go into advertising. Waiting tables and went to temp agency to find a job. She was hired as temp for Electronics Company and was working in finance and then worked her way up in sales to become manager.

How have you made choices about career and how did those decisions affect the way you balance marriage and children?

Career Choices/Decisions

Moved to big city different state to pursue career after college.
Never thought not to work.
I worked hard to get through college and wanted to move up in a company and knew I would work.
Hired as temp by Fortune 500 company and continued to work my way up the ladder in the company.
Moved into sales and then into management.
I worked long hours and was traveling flying and driving.
It never entered my mind that I would not work. I worked too hard to get to that point and move up into the company.

Career Path

It was easier when I was manager because I did not have to travel as much then as when I was a sales person. As a sales manager you are out in the thick of it. As a manager you do work longer hours because of different hours around the USA so you were the first and the last to leave.
I never thought I would get where I am today and have a successful career and move up in the company. I was lucky to be given the opportunities and I never planned the career just planned to work and work hard and have values and ethics.
I like work and I like to be busy and I like to move up and I liked to talk to directors anytime I wanted to and I was important.
I always stand up for myself and I could prove myself.
Work for me wasn't as much about the money but was to be valued.
I was the hard worker I believe in the work ethic and I believe you have to work hard and I will do it at every level yet those that are hard workers - hard work men or women and you can succeed and you can do it and many that worked for me are successful today.
I had great customers and found a way to get things done that worked for me
"Those that followed me hated my guts because I worked very hard for my clients and they appreciated it and would expect the next person to do the same.

Work Traits

Perfectionist
I do the job the best
I worked harder even when through into a position I did not know very well

I had great customers
I found a way... the things I was good at and found a way so it worked
Hard worker
Loved working and was good at it
Loved being a manager
Like being busy
Like my own money
Management style was hands on I had done all the jobs that my sales force did so I knew the tools that had and what was necessary to make their job successful. I had to fire a person and I had accounts calling me and I was fair for everybody and I understood it is demeaning to you if you cannot win a sales award if I was not fair and I always fought for my staff. And my staff did get used to doing things for them all the time. I enjoyed yet I ended up needing to move to make the next step to be a VP.

Career Effect on Family

Just assumed I could do it all. Most my friends outside of my work were all having kids and working just like me so we were together.
Planned to have children after 9 years of marriage. Won a top award while I was in the hospital having a baby and moving up in my company. "
I was working weekends and nights and traveling and pregnant
One manager indicated that I would not come back after pregnancy and I was so upset and I wrote it on a piece of paper and keep it because it made me angry that they would think it. I did get a manager's position and then during that I had a second child and I had men and one older woman. I was so busy working that I pumped milk while I was in the car. I was in the van and I was breast feeding child and otherwise I would pump and put it in the refrigerator. I had a room for pumping and it is the law to provide for mothers for 6 months. On the way home from work I would pump milk on the way home. I had someone watching child.
With my second child was 3 years later and I was a manager and it took awhile to get pregnant because we were both traveling.

Mentors and Advisors

I had great bosses that gave me opportunities
Difficult to have them as mentors since one of the few women with all men bosses
Few women and we were all concentrated on working and when not working and traveling being home to handle family. No women were at the level to be my mentor and it is different with men bosses.
Sometimes Managers would make you feel like you could lose your job and they put on you their concerns and it was put on you to do more and work harder and sometimes fear. Companies need to focus on value instead of fear.

<u>Support System</u>

My support system was my friends that had children also worked and we all helped each other. I never asked a stay at home mom because I believed they would not think good of me and I felt guilty. My mind set was I do not want to take advantage of stay at home moms. My support system was other women that had children and careers.

My husband was very supportive; we would look at our schedules and decide what was more important in our business so the other could be there if needed for the children. My husband was very supportive and he was traveling more yet he was very supportive and helped with all the activities at home.

How has career choices been an opportunity (enhancement) or conflict (loss) regarding marriage and children?

<u>Positive Spillover to Self</u>

Yes I was happier because I had a life outside of the home and I need it and I just had to be with adults

<u>Positive spillover to Marriage</u>

Career was a benefit for my husband – he was not the only provider and we are allowed the opportunity to take risk – both of us could. We had two incomes so what ever happened we were always OK

My husband and I shared and decided who had the most important meeting and we both would work together for our careers and our family priorities.

<u>Positive Spillover to Children</u>

Your kids are happy if you are happy. And when they are younger they are fine with someone to take care of them and they are in daycare and they need to be with other kids. It is a positive influence on the kids.

<u>Negative: Conflict to Children</u>

As the children get older it is more difficult to work because then they have activities after school and you cannot be there to help them. I did not have any help yet my husband and I shared in domestic and I am frugal and I can use that money for myself so for me I am wired differently than other people. My mom is different.

Everyone was telling I need to hire some help and it drove me crazy to have everyone telling men to hire help. Yet I had great kids and they were happy and were not in trouble and my husband and I would trade off.

As mothers we have the guilt and we as they are older it is more difficult. Then we need to be at their activities and we worry when they are eating on the run and not getting our attention.

As babies it is difficult for the women yet you do not think about it.

What sacrifices if any did you make in pursuing a career? What regrets if any do you have?

<u>Sacrifices to Self</u>

Loved my job and loved working and loved being a manager and I had make sacrifices because the next step up the ladder was to move and I did not want to move yet my husband was willing. I did not want to leave the city I was living in.
I did not take time for myself and I did not take care of myself.

<u>Sacrifices to Family</u>

Some, they had to eat fast food or whatever we could get quickly. I missed some of their activities and worried about them as they were getting older.

<u>Regrets</u>

No

<u>Advice to Younger Women</u>

I would tell them to find a career where they can work flexible hours so they could have marriage, children and work. Yet, make sure they find the job they love where they can have it all and be able to work their career with their children.

Jasmine

<u>Background</u>

Raised with family money, had a college education and wanted to have her own money and earn her own living. She did not want to work in the family business. She was one of the only females in the industry and the only female manager in the southwest at the Visitors Bureau

How have you made choices about career and how did those decisions affect the way you balance marriage and children?

<u>Career Choices/Decisions</u>

I wanted a career
I worked to get a college degree

Always worked and never thought not to work
I wanted my own money and my own success – not my family or the family business
Never thought about career as a choice just worked my way up the corporate ladder
Liked having my own money to spend as I want
Success allows independence
Always worked and was able to get the opportunity to move up the ladder and get promotions
Worked long hours; 12-14 hour days, nights and week ends
Traveled
Worked harder not smarter
My passion
My interest
Enjoyed working

Career Path

Never planned how far I would advance in my career just happened
Always needed to work
Blessed
Moved up the ladder
Worked harder not smarter
Always asked on promotions and took them
Never turned down an opportunity to take on more responsibility

Work Traits

Direct
Confident
Independent
Strong
Reliable
High Self Esteem
More comfortable with men – I have more common with them since we work together.
"I worked harder than other men". I worked 12-14 hour days, nights and weekends.
"In my time women still made less than men in the same career and I was told men would get paid more. Men did not have rules on how to treat a woman. They could make sexual remarks and sexual overtures and it was OK. Men would test me, read the paper in meetings, make sexual comments and it was OK. "
I trained men to take a promotion when I was more qualified. This was before laws and I was the token woman.
"It was up to me to set the standard for how I was treated as a manager and as a woman."
"I worked to make sure the men were comfortable working with me and accepted me based on my abilities, confidence and demand for respect and proper conduct".

Career Effect on Family

No effect
"I can do it all, it was what I did and I knew no difference"
Did not have children because unable to and just realized it was not meant to be.
No, always assumed I could do it all.
Never thought to plan or delay one for another.
Ponder decisions on family
Never did just met my first husband young married and realized it was not working out and then traveled with my job and focused on work. Later in my early 30s I met my current husband and married and worked the whole time and was a great wife and tried to have children yet was unable to have children.
"Children are scary". "Give me a board room and I am fine give me a 2 year old and I will be on my knees not knowing what to do…I will crumple".

Mentors and Advisors

None
Bosses gave me opportunities and chance at promotions yet not considered my mentor
Learned on my own

Support System

Support system was my husband
Support system was independent people. Even women I know that are married and have children are independent and work like me and have strong character.
My women friends work and do not have children. So the children stuff is scary.
I was with the men I worked with and had more in common with them then with their wife or with other women that stayed home and had children.
How has career choices been an opportunity (enhancement) or conflict (loss) regarding marriage and children?

Positive Spillover

Yes
Driven
Independent
Financial independent – I had my own money
Self esteem
Who I am
Confidence
Credibility

Positive Spillover to Marriage

Yes

"My husband married a woman that had a title, a powerful woman and that is what I offered to my husband"

I could communicate

I was social

I would handle any situation

I could understand his business and work to help his business.

Positive from career to husband and step children. Work was my life and I just did not thing about it. When I met my husband I was older and already successful in my own in career. I never turned down a promotion, worded hard to move up the ladder and never contemplated whether it was the right thing to do.

Positive Spillover to Children

Yes

Positive to the step children

Handle situations as they arose

I took care of step children and I packed when I moved and I did not know what not to do. I was an enabler. I just did things to take care and get it done.

What sacrifices if any did you make in pursuing a career? What regrets if any do you have?

Sacrifices to Self

None

Sacrifices to Family

None

Regrets

No

Advice to Younger Women

Balancing is important, work because it is my life and it was the most important thing and I did not balance my personal identity. You need to balance early on because I was strange I worked and I never knew to do anything else. Today hopefully women are at a place where they can have it all and they can balance by knowing who they are in the beginning and to have their own self worth and then know your good and bad traits so you can work it into your life and work it into your schedule. So you can have marriage and children with a career. Now a days they did not have to fight to be a woman they have that this is a new generation and may be able to work 8-5 pm and get it done. I worked until 8 or 9 pm working 14 hour days and Sundays were normal. Woman can do it all and they are equal we did that so hopefully we paved the way for them so they are equal for the most part and now fan have it all and balance work with marriage and children.

Kayla

Background

She had a strong dad that was her mentor and a stay at home mom. She is a college theatre degree and broadcasting degree two bachelors and ended up in TV on the technical side then editing and then the post production and behind the scenes with production.

How have you made choices about career and how did those decisions affect the way you balance marriage and children?

Career Choices/Decisions

In a simple concept I tell my children it is like baking a cake; you need to management all the ingredients and watch the temperature and make sure "you do it all".
I always assumed I would have a career.
I worked hard at college and had a double major.
Never thought not to work
It never entered my mind that I would not work. I worked too hard to get to that point and move up into the company.
I loved what I did best part was when I worked as director for advertising agency and became executive producer.
Great jobs
Great opportunities
Career path
Two bachelors and ended up in TV on the technical side then editing and then the post production behind the scenes stuff.

On the TV and post production side realized I wanted to be in the advertising side since they did get the free lunches and so I ended up succeeding at it as a director of a major advertising agency as they merged with another company I had more opportunities.

This is when I became executive producer and it was the most fun part of my career and I had 8-15 projects TV, radio, events, all were great jobs and great opportunities and I loved my job.

Work Traits

Independent
Direct
Strong
Control Freak
High Energy
High activity
Self esteem
Be the best at every stage of the game.
Loved working and loved being a manager
Set priorities and do what you have to do.

Career Effect on Family

I always wanted to have a child. I tried with my first husband and it did not happen. So
when I was married in my 30s and was pregnant I was thrilled – I was established in my
career and wanted a child.
I just assumed I could do it all.
You just make sure you juggle it all.
Worked long hours and week ends
When I had my first child I worked and would take her with me.
Would take my child to work on the weekends
Mentors and advisors
No mentors, good bosses no mentors learned on my own.
I just worked hard and moved up the ladder.

Support System

I had a nanny and someone to help out. Mothers want to make sure you have a good
nanny or caretaker and I went through 5 nannies. Yet it took many nannies and still there
is guilt

**How has career choices been an opportunity (enhancement) or conflict (loss)
regarding marriage and children?**

Positive Spillover to Self

Yes I was happier because I had a life outside of the home and I need to work.
I stayed home for 8 months and was crazy and had to go back to work.
Never wanted to leave my job.

Work is easier, children are more difficult You have to make choices and you have to
decide what to do with the children. I would take a baby with me in meetings on
weekends, I was the top person and in charge so I did not ask I just did it. I was in chargeof
everything and no one said a word since I always completed the production. When I
traveled I would have my husband take care of the children.

Positive Spillover to Marriage

Career was a benefit for my husband – he was not the only provider and we are allowed the opportunity to take risk – both of us could. We had two incomes so what ever happened we were always OK.

If I was happy he was happy when I stayed home he knew I needed to go back to work. Men are attracted to successful women.

Positive Spillover to Children

Your kids are happy if you are happy. And when they are younger they are fine with someone to take care of them and they are in daycare and they need to be with other kids. It is a positive influence on the kids.

Negative: Conflict to Self

No, career was wonderful yet with a blended family and a husband that is CEO it was difficult time.

Children are easier when they are younger – more difficult when they are teenagers.

I am doing more and juggling. We have to make choices and juggle schedules and set priorities.

Negative: Conflict to Husband

Must be or we were worried about me because he told me when he was making more than our combined income that I could have the choice of staying home with the children or working part time.

Negative: Conflict to Children

As mothers we have the guilt and we as they are older as teenagers it is more difficult.

Sacrifices to Self

Yes, I left my career for 8 months and I was never so miserable.

It just was not for me to stay home and not work.

Yes, just do what you have to do. All my women friends are strong and in control women. We as women at our age whom pursued careers always worked. Men and women are wired differently – it is just the way it is.

Woman's movement is great yet it was also a burden; we had to make sacrifices and live up to the movement that we can do it all. Yes, decided to start my own company. Now I can control what I do and decide it is OK

to do my own thing. I used my resource of people to build up the company. I have the skills and the contacts to run my own business.

Have time for me and to pursue my own business. When my last child is 18; "it is time for me to pursue my goals and my game to the maximum at my company…this is my opportunity to be the best I can be at every stage of the game".

Sacrifices to Family

Only when the children were older teenagers are more difficult to make sure they have the guidance and could not always attend their activities.
We are the nurtures: I have to be there for my children .There is the struggle for all executive women we have to sacrifice the career or the husband or the children. It is part of the guilt makeup.

Regrets

No

Advice to Younger Women

We as executive women at our age always worked and were in control and today women may be the same because women have changed yet men have not changed.
Today I see more women that have the money and they make the money. Hopefully women today will have more options to work fewer hours and work from their home. I believe I could have worked from my home yet it was work in the office or you will not have a job. The internet technology will change the opportunity for both men and women the next generation to work out of the home and have more flexibility for their family. Women are getting more degrees and so with those changes women as much or more as their husbands.

Megan

Background
She has 25 years in the banking business. She has a college degree and has strong parents

How have you made choices about career and how did those decisions affect the way you balance marriage and children? Career Choices/Decisions

Out of college did not know what I wanted to do. I had the perfect blend of analytical and relationship business. Stayed in the banking business for 25 years.
College students have difficulty choosing careers and companies. You are clueless…you can tell the kids that have been coached and those that have not been in business world and I do not know how to .
Dad was influential to my career – needed the shove to push me over. My parents were college educated. My mom said you cannot be a nurse because you cannot be sub servant. Strong parents.

Career Path

I started out in training program and my boyfriend now husband did not want to move to

Houston so compromise was Dallas he wanted to be in Austin. I worked long hours and days in the business to be the best at what job I was working. Male dominated industry. Only one other woman in role and it was in private banking so I did not want to go into female area.

Very few women in the industry – even today there is a small number of women in the business in the Midwest which should be even more progressive than the South.

I have a male mentor that was my boss.

I have to be here yet I am at the level of being able to do my own thing. I have the presence because of the level I am at.

Work Traits

Strong
Direct
Aggressive
"Be the best you can in the job you have not the job you want to have"
In a male dominated career more like the men then other women that do not work.

Career Effect on Family

Never planned career, or children – never a question, I just thought I would figure it out. First kid I was not a manager, with the 2nd kid I was a manager and moved up to supervisor and I had to go through the mindset am I prepared to derail my career for my family. Yet, I did go to my boss and I said I will take a 20% cut in salary and work 4 days – worked 10-12 hours a day and it was worth it yet I was getting more done and I was at story hour. Yet then I was promoted and it was with my mentor and he knew I could do this. My boss promoted me as he was promoted. I tell young women be the best you can be in the job that you are in – we have a open culture to promote within the company and all the people you a hand in their success. I had one person that mentored me. I did go to him and said I love what I do but I am bored. I had a call to run the trust department and it was a big stepping stone I managed over 80 people in 4 locations and had to fire people and I had both kids. Then I ran this department until I was ready for a new challenge. I did go to higher level job and I said here is what I want to do. And he said move and I said no and he said it is OK and then you are out of the roles and you have to move. So then I decided I did not want to move and I want to stay in this city and you better talk to her before she leaves and she is the one for this job.

Mentors and Advisors

My boss

How as career choices been an opportunity (enhancement) or conflict (loss) regarding marriage and children?

Positive Spillover to Self

The work for me is easier when they are older, yet I have good kids. I have had nannies and I had a stay a home mom that we paid and she was my neighbor and she also cooked. My son said I am going through a process that I was gone more nights and I am gone at least 2 nights.
I live in the moment – I do think about future I cannot imagine not working My husband would be ready for me to slow down I see another crisis coming in the future…I cannot see myself not working.
As you move into higher level positions you have more flexibility because people work for you.

Positive Spillover to Marriage

Career is as benefit to my husband. My husband moved his office home after 5-6 nannies and mental breakdown and stressed and he moved home and took on 20% less clients. Husband should be equal in the home to help out. We as women and men have traditional roles – in the house my mom used to run the house yet I am not around to do that so he has to help out. We had "traditional" values yet my mom ran the house and we reported to my "mom" and I cannot do that I cannot run the house alone.

My husband tells me "he loves me in spite of your job". He does not care where I work. The balance of powers is important. It is important to me for both of us to have an equal stake in financial. In the last 10 years I made more money. I was careful that he was He said I do not need to work – I said you need to work. I like the balance of power. Husband & I balance with kids. My 2nd son was born, I lost my father and we had a difficult time. I had to ask my husband to help and to do things. Instead of talking about it I just was madder and I was more aggressive and he becomes more passive aggressive and we had to figure it out. I felt like he was helping me out with the kids, yet I never vocalized. 103
Positive Spillover to Children

Career is a benefit for my children. It is a benefit. They may not realize it but it is a benefit. I had a presentation on work/family balance so I did research. So I explained concept a 1 – 10 (10 is a 100) what grade to you give me.

My older son said I give you a 70 on that is average. That is a C – what would make me get a 90 or 100. I was braced for the guilt trip. "He said Mom you talk to me like I work for you and if you did not use all these work words and you did treat me like I work for you then you would be a 90". Average is not acceptable for a driven type A personality. I said what can I do? – if you would not treat me like an employee. I said thank you for the feedback and he said that is my point – you treat me like an employee you just did it see that is one of those words. My 2nd son said I give you an 80 and what can I do to get 90 and he said "I would like you around".

Children see work comes first yet I want them to know they come first and I started having breakfast with my children on Fridays until my one son said sleep is more important than breakfast. I am trying to be there more for them and make them know they are first.

What sacrifices if any did you make in pursuing a career? What regrets if any do you have?

Sacrifices to Self

I do not take time for myself; accept for running and Yoga on Saturday.

My women friends, I have not cultivated friends if we are not doing something for work then I would rather be home and relax. I like type A types and I do not look down on stay at home moms – I think I am intimating to them. I have more in common with the ones working – "you are so smart and I cannot keep up with it" stay at home mom.

It is hard for them to be around me as they are difficult with me.

I drifted over to the guys because I understand them better and have more in common with them".

Regrets

No

Advice to Younger Women

I try to be very realistic – 50% of the women are able to contain in the business at the professional level. At the professional level they have to work the hours and be in the office. I think the next generation if you get through the first 10 years at work and you have kids older then you can wait and it will be easier. I can work 24 hours a day with a computer and cell phone – in our day we could not do that. Hopefully my kids will not know that it is traditional for women to cook at home they like to cook and they are boys

Nora

Background

She is in the research business and worked up to sales management. She moved into different sales positions until she found a natural fit. Her interest was always sales and sales management. She always worked even in college. She has a college education as does both her parents.

How have you made choices about career and how did those decisions affect the way you balance marriage and children?

Career Choices/Decisions

Never considered I would not work. Always thought I would work. Worked through college and was hired by the career woman that was my supervisor in college. She helped me get another job because she introduced me to a company and I ended up in sales. I was single and was successful in sales and continued to be promoted.
The first change of job was demanded because of getting married and while manager did not have a territory in Austin and then I took another and it was a Dallas territory and work that with a husband and a new house and work in Dallas all week and then arrive Friday at 8pm and nothing was done to put the house together.
Only when I felt devalued by a company, I did reach a point of frustration at my corporation with their management style and did decide then give to my children and give to my other responsibilities.
I did not want to give up the money I was making so much money.
I made a great change to be valued. I did not feel valued – I was devalued – the company made me feel I was devalued and that was why I left and went with another company it was never an issue of my family.
I was a sales manager and then a director of sales both roles where I traveled yet the easiest position for me was as a sales manager; I could direct and guide people.

Career Path

Never considered not to work.
I was programmed that way – to work.
I always worked throughout my years of marriage.
You just do the best job and opportunities occur.
I was the top in my company and appreciated the money and the life style.
Did not know I would be as successful as it turned out.
I never have ridden down goals, I never really planned.
Sales fit into my personality and I was driven to do the absolute best.

Sales were a normal and natural career for me and then I moved from sales to management.
I could give advice to those that worked for me on what I had accomplished in sales.
You just go out and work and do what you need to move up in the company.
So in management you are giving guidance and direction.
Continued to take promotions and be promoted.
Always worked hard and focused on doing the best job.
Moved up the ladder
I always needed to work since it was a part of me.
It is your results and numbers that tell your story on what you did – I just went out and take it. I only would see my manager once a month and then once a quarter – it was based on numbers and a phone call to find out how you did.
You have to spend the time traveling and working I did that for about 10 years single prior to getting married and having children.

Work Traits

Direct
Aggressive
Focused
Independent
Competitive
Driven to be the best
Results are based on your numbers
Objective
Determined
Take charge
Prefer to work with men – more like them and less jealous
I absolutely enjoy work and I enjoy people. I justified that I have been given the skills and gift and the passion to be given the skills to work and not question that I could do both and I had great people to help.
I have faith.

Career Effect on Family

I assumed I could do it all
I never had a strong need to nurture.
Assumed you would marry and have children.
I had a nanny and help with the children.
Your kids may not turn out exactly like you want yet you do not pick your kids it is not utopia.
I am programmed a certain way and work is part of that program.
I took management positions to allow more time at home with the children. Interview for Pharmaceutical sales and where do you see yourself in 10 years and I said having a happy family. So there was a desire to have a family unit that was functional. I worked up to the

day I had the baby and did not want children to have until after 30 and I let God make the choice for me and I was pregnant and I was ok with it there is a lot of challenges with kids and I have grown more in that area and yet they have not turned out exactly like I wanted yet you do not get to pick your kids it is not a utopia. At lot of my friends do have time passage and then decide later if they want a child. Having a child is the desire to nurture. I never had a strong need for nurturing – it was strong in faith and I am, programmed a certain way.

After the first 10 years it is easier as you move to higher level positions.

Mentors and Advisors

Women failed to mentor other women. I still believe that is true although I was in a male dominated industry. We as women are our own worst enemies because of jealousy in the industry and competition with other women.

I had one woman mentor out of college. My woman mentor had the view you can do what you want to do and she commanded respect from men and she was a take charge woman and that is what I did too. I was an outside sales rep and had to work independently.

All the rest of my mentors were men – one manager was significant in my life and key to my decisions

Support System

I choose that church because they did not ask me how many kids I had and they had kids and I didn't and most in my age bracket started early. Most of the stay at home moms through church was there when I had my baby and helped because my husband was not home. We lived in different cities.

No family in the city where I lived so you have to depend on others. I had a neighbor stay at home mom and they liked to be at my house. The kids were instrumental meeting the parents and I hired the mom to be my assistant. When you spend time with another woman you have common paths and common interests.

I had minimum contact with stay at home moms.

How has career choices been an opportunity (enhancement) or conflict (loss) regarding marriage and children?

Positive Spillover to Self

Yes although companies need to know that being valued is very important. If you are undervalued or company rules by fear then you will move to another company even if it is for less money. The positive success allows you these options.

Positive Spillover to Marriage

There was some resentment for me when I felt I was taking on more responsibilities with the children than him. He needed to share equally and understand.

Positive Spillover to Children

You would have to ask my children since they are older now. My daughter is strong and
independent like me. Work traits were positive spillover to my children, yet especially to
my daughter since she has the same traits and is independent and sees career as a benefit
to her life.
I wanted to have a functional family unit.
There are a lot of challenges with kids yet you can just do the best you can.

Negative: Conflict to Marriage

I am sure I felt short in different areas yet am a good balance and we made it work. My
husband was based in Dallas and we lived in Atlanta and I had a full time person living
with me. And I could work the hours I wanted to work.

Negative: Conflict to Children

There is the feeling that if I had stayed at home with my son he would have been different. There is the guilt.

**What sacrifices if any did you make in pursuing a career? What regrets if any do
you have?**

Sacrifices to Self

I had to move for husbands new assignments. I was planning to move to Austin and
needed to move 4-5 months early and I had huge bonuses; he said fine yet did not keep
his promise and hired a man for the job. I was the 5th woman hired and the youngest
person; I only called on 3 women; every partner or every law firm and every CPA firm
were men. My husband and I often lived in separate cities yet made sure our companies
could be close to drive 4 ok with a strong independent woman.
Usually I dated older men yet my husband was the same age is me and he was ok with
my independence. Men are intimated by strong women. Women cannot change

they are
who they are who I am today; my daughter doesn't date and she is very strong and very
driven and is not the dating kind.

Regrets
vice to Younger Women

I would be interested to ask my daughter would you have liked your mom to do it differently. Do they see it differently? Are they able to work less hours today then we did in our generation.
Men can be intimated by strong powerful women – hopefully that will change.

Ruby

How have you made choices about career and how did those decisions affect the way you balance marriage and children?

Background

She is a corporate executive in the health care industry. She has a college education She worked her way up the ladder to become part owner of a health company division.

Career Choices/Decisions

I wanted a career.
I always planned to work.
I was a corporate executive
Worked for Fortune 100 Company
I was the only woman in the business and helped to build the company.
I made a name –I had to fit into a culture that did not respect women.
I proved my way with them.
I just found opportunities.
The first, I have no fear.
Promoted ran national contracts.
I moved as needed to different cities as required for job promotions.

Career Path

Always planned to work and never turned down an opportunity or a promotion.
Love working it is my passion makes me who I am today
I love to travel, modify my like family and roots.
In fact, many times attempted to work less yet could not turn down an opportunity.
More money and prestige

The value of relationships in business allows you to learn how to cope and deal with what needs to be handled whether at work or at home
and knowledge and the opportunities to grow.
I could not have had my success without this being corporate America and the opportunities. 109

Work Traits

Independent
Driven
No Fear
Confident
Strong
High Self Esteem
Compensate
Fit into a man world
You become one of the guys.
It is emotional yet you do not show your emotions. You have to hold back and they do
not get it like we do – we understand.
"Cram the square peg into the round hole" "Somehow we make it fit and it becomes part
of us and who we are".
"As women you can guide us and then the problem is they (the men) want to mold us into
his mindset of doing things a certain way. It doesn't work for me to do business because
they want me and what is unique to me and I want to do things my way"
If this continues then women will leave and start their own companies.

Career Effect on Family

It just is.
I was the only female in the executive team.
Just like the others you see your co workers more than your family ... "sent our spouses
Christmas cards of us because we did not see them one year". .
You go you are accustomed to doing it and I just do it I get up at 6am and I do the same
thing and I make sure everyone is doing what they have to do it is not that hard.
It is timing all is about timing. You just do it and it is part of my esteem no way that I
will not have a career.
Difficult to shut off your business sense it is how you run things at home.
Guilt is always an issue with mothers. They are easier when they are younger as long as
you find a good caretaker or nanny.
The domestic issues can be resolved – hire someone competent and then you have quality

time with the children at home.

"Once I was in my 30s I wanted to be married and have children. So that is what I did. I

knew it was time to add the family life in my life.

I married to have children.

I assumed I could do it all. I waited later in life to marry so I wanted to have kids right

away.

No, I was going to take a break did not happen – let me ride my ride. And why would I

not want to do it and I made a lot of money and why would I not want to do it. Fortune

500 company,

I had a great nanny, lady that kept kids in home. Then I moved them to daycare.

110

I never asked for anything, never for a promotion or a step up just worked hard and this is what I do and have to do - it is for me!

Structure, your time and make it work

I tried to leave one company since my children as teenagers needed me around yet they asked me to stay and gave me stock and money to stay.

Mentors and Advisors

No mentors

My supervisors were advisors and offered opportunities for me to take continued promotions.

I was often asked by my bosses for my advice and influence into the team.

Support System

Friends in the business

Women Friends

How has career choices been an opportunity (enhancement) or conflict (loss) regarding marriage and children?

Positive Spillover to Self

Yes, It is who I am

It is right for me

I do what I loved to do and I am passionate about.

It will allow more opportunities in future – maybe have own business, have flexibility and control to make decisions. Focus more on commuting giving and reaching out to other women.

Positive Spillover to Marriage

It needs to be a positive spillover to your marriage. If it is not then change it.

If a relationship is too much work it is not worth it.

"Why fix what is not broken" You can be divorced have a relationship with your ex that is positive to the children.

If you have to fix it then it is not right.

I want it to work now.

I have a lot of guy friends and I want to enjoy my life.

"At this point I do not want to have someone in my life"

That may change when it is the right person down the road yet it is not critical for my esteem and success.

Financial advantage is a benefit to the spouse and to the marriage less stress should be placed on the relationship. 111

<u>Positive: Opportunity to Children</u>

Resilience - Kids weather all the storms. Ex husband stays with kids and my older kids

pick up their responsibilities to pick up the slack and do what they have to do they are so

conscientious. As they are teenagers you need to make sure they are in the right direction.

It all worked out my kids are good and working.

<u>Negative: Conflict to Marriage</u>

When it is work with the marriage then there is conflict, so you need to get rid of the

negative or the conflict.

There is resentment when you work and you feel you are carrying the load of the children. The husband sees it as helping you, but when I was home it is your turn– work

together to get it done – he never traveled and I was working. He wanted to have his guy

time; seeing friends, hunting, fishing, golf with guys. He needs to give up some of his

time. Concept is husband is a good father yet there is resentment for the woman that

builds up.

She will not see her friends yet does not ask the husband just gets resentful. There was no

us time. If husband underachiever in career AND does not give up for the children then it

does not work and women say I can do it alone.

<u>Sacrifices to Self</u>

No

<u>Sacrifices to Family</u>

No
Regrets

No

<u>Advice to Younger Women</u>

Men and women are wired differently
Think of it as a chest of drawers; each drawer – career, personal, children and we multi
task and men compartmentalize.
Determine who you can live with and who you can live without, what you can live with
and what you can live without.
The next generation will not be as successful as us. They will have less and do less and
have fewer opportunities due to the economy. They will deal with adversity and challenges and will have a difficult time realizing they will not provide for their children
like we did for our children. 112
Sophie

<u>Background</u>

She has a graphic design degree; creative color, structure, visual implementation. She worked her way up in the retail industry. She ended up working as Vice President for large jewelry company. She has worked as a Supervisor for 25 years. She has 40 people that report to her.

How have you made choices about career and how did those decisions affect the way you balance marriage and children?

<u>Career Choices/Decisions</u>

Career was a choice, at least I wanted to work and move up in a career.
I graduated and moved to Dallas to get job in design at an advertising agency Yet I ended up working in a totally different field, landed a job at Dallas Apparel Mart – furniture creative division; learned a lot most from this company; manager left and I took over and had no experience in management. Work with vendors visit people from all over the country. One year and then a manager – that job taught me enough that I wanted to manage people
Decided to get my Masters and wanted to be a teacher. Then ended up back in the business world since my supervisor called to offer me a job. My strength is the ability to pull the team together.

<u>Career Path</u>

I worked in different companies – design worked my way up the ladder

Attention to detail – visual how design and structure relate to anything

Would help out with any job

I was younger and learned from others

While I was married worked and went back to school to get my Masters to have more opportunities

I never planned it – I thought I want to be a teacher or graphic designer. I worked my way up and it was all about serving people – guide them functions are different theme of in authority where people ask you for advice how to gain customers and built relationships and it is my strength and it comes out. I am not looking for the next promotion it has just come up. Every promotion I have though do I want to take the extra promotion, yet my mentor helped me and I could not turn down the job. I found them generous and I was fortunate to get the promotion and have someone who is my boss let me decide where I would work.

Supervisor of 25 employees

I think people are interesting and I enjoy men and women and their personalities.

Company is diverse and attracts a diverse group of people and allows me to interface with a mix of people because that is who are company is.

Work Traits

Control

Multitasking

Manage people

Attention to detail

Professionalism

Direct

No nonsense

Practically more than emotions

Hard worker – work with your employees

Set an example

Team focused

Softer version of men

Creativity

Career Effect on Family

Just did it.

No, my husband and I have a great balance. Before kids was more challenging because it

was the kids that forced us to be together. We are both career driven and as soon as we

had kids we need to be home more and change our priorities. My husband is there doing

what I need – his job allows for flexibility. He is the type of person that is so willing and

he stayed home and watched the kids on weekends for many years. In general I do work

weekends because it is best for the business. He knows they are his children as mine. He

will cook, play with the kids and focus on what needs to get done. When he is home he

cooks and when not nanny does it. I struggled for a long time that I wanted to be there for

dinner. I get the up extra early so we can have breakfast together. I have all organized the

night before.

Women are wired differently.

Then we opened another store planned my pregnancy and first time was pregnant; I was

so comfortable at this place and knew I would stay and my friends were having children

and it seemed like the right time. I worked to end and then had baby came back worked 3

years had another child and did the same thing. I changed my hours and my routine but I

was in a position and a level to be able to do so. My husband travels all the time and he

was gone Monday through Thursday so I had a lot of responsibility here – yet I felt like a

single mom and we were open on the week end. Every week my husband was the dad on

duty I had Friday as my day off and Sunday we alternate. I have a babysitter for 6 years.

Mentors and Advisors

My women supervisors in some of my jobs were my mentors

My last woman boss was my mentor and guided me in my success in the corporation.

I prefer working with women as supervisor

People just recommended me and as a mentor they moved me along. It has been 10 years with the same company. I started as sales manager and am director.

My boss moved on to another company. She said she was not leaving unless I go and I worshipped her and knew she was working for my best interest. I was afraid to job hop and I always trusted her and she was always loyal and looking out for me. So I decided to interview and I liked it and knew I could grow the business and it seemed like a good thing and I was offered the position and accepted it and of course she accepted it too. She interviewed for a company and told me about it; all was well yet there were changes that were going and she realized conflicts were arising and I knew my boss was going to leave. I felt I should leave or watch for opportunities. She took another job and she met with my current boss and they had dinner told her about the sales manager position yet salary was too low for her and her experience and so she told the interviewee I have a little gift for you and I have her resume and yet I never had applied for a job.

Support System

Husband
Positive and I have a husband that helps and is there doing what I need him to do.

Balance

My time was divided by work and two children far different from work and one child yet working and making more money allowed me to provide more for them to give more for their education. And when I thought about not taking the promotion I knew it could be me and I was good and I did not want to report to another person. I knew the position and could do the job and did not want to give that up.
Having the ability to make decisions and do what is right for the store and I can do it. Worked hard good at what I did (never a word about competition).

How has career choices been an opportunity (enhancement) or conflict (loss) regarding marriage and children?

Positive Spillover to Self

Yes

Positive Spillover to Marriage

Husband – He is very supportive of my career. He helps out. He is more free going even though he has a serious career. He is his own business owner. I feel like I have more responsibilities and bring work home. I am the more structured than him he is the fun enjoying have a good time. I am more stressed and I have to take more work home.
Positive Spillover to Children

Overall, I hear different philosophies, I think I am setting a good example for my girls
whether level they take it serious realize it is a project their minds are forming and they
take responsible for their actions and they see they need to be responsible and complete
tasks.
Independent
Responsible
Complete tasks

Negative: Conflict to Self

Every woman with a career is the last person on the list is herself. Yet, I do take time for
my girlfriends at least once a month and that is important to me. I feel guilty that it is the

one time I am home from traveling, yet I believe if you cannot be a good friend you

cannot have a good friend.

<u>Negative: Conflict to Children</u>

Miss some of their activities.

**What sacrifices if any did you make in pursuing a career? What regrets if any do
you have?**

<u>Sacrifices to Self</u>

Every women last person on the list is herself; yet I do take time for my girlfriends. At
least 3-4 there and that is important for me. I feel guilty that it is the one time I am home
from traveling. Yet I believe if you cannot be a good friend you cannot have a good
friend.
I have learned the last several years that I have to say no to my family and friends not my
work, prior to that I said yes to friends and family. I work so hard I need to say no to my
family and friends so we can have our own Christmas and events.

<u>Sacrifices to Family</u>

Yes, when they were younger they did not know and as long as they were taken care of it
was fine. As they get older it is more difficult. They did call me mom and would be with
me even with the nanny. I would get home at 6 or 7 at night so our time was quality time;
laundry, dishes done all of our time was playing and talking except my days off. We had
our time to do fun things. I think that is what created our strong bond. Now children want
me to be there for all activities; she wants me to come and be at lunch concert – I have to
pick and choose due to my work. There are times when I cannot do things like that and
she has cried and the majority of the moms don't work – so that is what she sees moms at
school all the time. Other moms will take them, yet I have someone to take care
of them nd choosing right person is important. And nanny needs to help with homework and do
things that are more challenging. Girls started school they need to have help and I can

only check and go over; I need their homework done. I sometimes get home at 8pm at night.

Regrets

No I do not think I cannot work – I look at friends and family that do not work I can imagine it I do not know something is in me I have to work I feel the need to work I thought about it when I had the children. I choose not to stay home; couple of different reasons – reason I did not want to work part time is because of financial yet the answer was no it is part of me controlling

Advice to Younger Women

To find what makes you happy and work towards that and not to wait or someone will provide for me and to be independent and not to rely on someone to be financial or emotionally dependent. Do what drives you and work hard and if you have an opportunity to stay home fine yet I have chosen a different time. Some kids cling to their mothers and takes time to take to the school they are crying because they are so upset mine are used to me getting up and leaving and I will put them in the hands of someone I trust and I think the example I am setting for the girls is the right one. And my children are young yet in the future they will be in college and gone and what would I do entering a career later after I leave it because it would be difficult for me because I am at a level that I have reached financially and emotionally. Focus more on women reaching out to women

Violet

Background

She attended college while working fulltime and married. She worked completed her Masters degree to work her way up from a secretary to Management in a Manufacturing Company.

How have you made choices about career and how did those decisions affect the way you balance marriage and children?

Career Choices/Decisions

Assumed I would be a secretary and then I was bored because my husband was traveling and I decided to attend school to get a college degree. Then I was able to get a job in a bank that was my dream job. I moved up the company and then was hired by the Company I wanted to work there. Little by little I worked my way up in this company. I worked and attended school; Thur.-Sun. I continued to get promotions and was promoted for 13 years. I was naïve and thought I could do what the managers were doing.

I was told I could get promoted if I had a Masters so I did get a Masters and felt betrayed because I did not get the promotion to management. Get your masters was the carrot and I did it and did not get promoted. There was a $40,000 difference in my job and job with masters. Yet, after I obtained my masters I was told I need line experience. I felt betrayed.

I decided to bid for new jobs.

I did not feel valued. Value in a company is important sometimes money is a reflection of value if you are doing the same work and feel you are significantly underpaid.

It was at the time I was looking for new company that I ended up pregnant. I was on maternity leave when I decided to ask for a raise.

Met a man that I wanted to work for and applied for the job and received it when I returned from maternity leave. He was my mentor and I learned much about business and teams from this person.

Career Path

Never planned my career; my mother just told me to take care of myself.

Staying home was not part of my makeup

I enjoy working

Even with successful husband I could not stay home it was not part of my makeup.

I would seek promotions and looked around at people in management and said I can do that

Always asked how to move up the ladder, what I needed, what I could do.

Being valued in a company is most important.

Yet, we need to make money too. Resented it when men doing the same job were making more than me some over $40,000

Work Traits

Aggressive

Strong

Bulldozer

Competitive

Thrive on constructive feedback

Give me an objective and I will nail it down.

Career Effect on Family

Just assumed I would be able to handle it all.

I did not want to give up my career.

Pregnant was just like any other project, I handled it like every other project.

I am trying to do it all

I was married young and was bored while he was traveling I just worked and kept attending school at night.

I just cannot stay at home – it is not my makeup.

Mentors and advisors

I had one supervisor after I had moved up a long time in the company who was my mentor and is still my friend today.

Prior to that time I had advocates, they knew I worked hard and said if you wanted done give it to her.

Never had someone say these are the land mines to avoid.

Support System

My husband
My girlfriends

How has career choice been an opportunity (enhancement) or conflict (loss) regarding marriage and children?

Positive Spillover to Self

When my life was simple it was fine

It was more complex such as adding children. One child was easier than two,

It was easier to juggle two balls verses 3 balls or twirling plates the more to juggle more plates is more complex and complicates the situation. I had too many balls in the air.

You have to plan to manage more projects.

Positive Spillover to Marriage

We both have careers and we were proud of it. I enjoyed my career and we made it work. It helps on the financial responsibility and gives you both more options.

Working is positive to marriage, being together a long time is difficult in any marriage yet it is no related to career. And then because I had been with my husband for so long you look at that relationship and do I still love him and do I want to work on it – come on it is work in a marriage and the longer you are together the more you have to do to keep it exciting.

Positive Spillover to Children

Independence
They know the purpose of working119
Negative: Conflict to Children

Missed their events – felt guilty

I depended on the stay at home mothers to keep me update of school events and activities.

I was traveling and busy with work.

What sacrifices if any did you make in pursuing a career? What regrets if any do

you have?

Sacrifices to Self

I was doing a good job at everything. I was not great and that was what bothered me. I was to throw a great party not a good party; I want to be a great wife not a good wife; I want to be a great employee not a good employee, I want to be a great mom not a good mom. I was doing everything good not great.

No time for friends. My friends were working women like me usually in couples due to the lack of time to be separate from my husband so very little time outside of family and couple friends.

Sacrifices to Family

I was always packed and ready to travel with my business – one day I arrived home to pick up my luggage that was already packed and ready to go and my 3 year old child was seated on the top of my luggage and she said mom stay with me please don't go…that was a turning point where I realized how much I was traveling and away from my child.

Regrets

No

Advice to Younger Women

I think the most important thing you need is a great network – your own personal network people that you trust and are not like you and those that will hug you and those that want hug you and say you think you have problems let's go to the children floor with those that are dying. There are highs and lows and I do not think we can figure it out by ourselves we need fabulous women to help us. I love my husband and plan to spend my life with him. He is a great husband, business partner and lover yet sometimes I need a great woman friend, listen, I believe you become the 5 people you hang with. You need dream builders not dream drainers in your girlfriends. You need a network of women that will give you support and give to you and you have to give to them.

Women experts are different that they are women and they need other women. The biggest seat when you are in the captain seat you has the moral obligation to give back and I have a project that is giving back and involves women. GROUP TEXTURAL DESCRIPTION

Summary of group responses with the same message which lead to the themes discussed

How have you made choices about career and how did those decisions affect the way you balance marriage and children?

Theme: I never thought not to work

Career Choices/Decisions

Never thought not to work
Wanted a career
Never planned my success
Good at what I did and was promoted for abilities
Never left a meeting to pick up a child
Loved working, loved the opportunity to move up the ladder
Never turn down a promotion, seek promotions and take on more responsibility
Worked long hours
I did not want to give up the money and success
Some luck – right place at the right time
Lots of hard work; be the best you can in current position

Work Traits

Reliable
Strong, aggressive
Take charge
Independent
Competitive
High Energy
Confident, self esteem
Worked hard, visible to company
Enjoyed managing people
Set priorities and manage
Multitasking

How have career choices been an opportunity (enhancement) or loss (conflict) regarding marriage and children?

Theme: Career is a positive influence on self.

Career is a benefit; self esteem identity, confidence, empowerment, purpose, prestige, a priority.
Career is security, value and happiness.
Career gives you financial stability.
Career gives you opportunity to make choices.
Who I am and what I do.

Theme: Career is a positive influence on marriage

Overall message career was a benefit to their husband.
Both working allows financial security.
We are both allowed the opportunity to take risks.
Need a supportive husband to make it work.
Set work and home priorities.
Positive when you are successful and you can help each other in business.

Need to share in responsibilities – work and home when it was in conflict then resulted in divorce.

Husband was a positive support in a successful marriage (seemed if not supportive then they would be a single mom).

Theme: Career is a positive influence on children

Contribution to their children: independence, responsibility, and resilience.
Children knew benefit of parents as providers.
Children realize at they need to be independent.
Children learn to socialize at a young age since they were in daycare.
Your kids are happy if you are happy.
They make sure they have quality time with their children.
Children were aware of time management and had to manage their own time.
As moved up ladder they were able to have domestic help and nannies.

Theme: Career responsibilities contribute to maternal guilt

All mothers admit there are "guilt" feelings with their children, yet executive women indicated it occurs with stay at home moms too.
"Guilt" seems to be a universal trait of women with their children.
You worry about them eating right and staying on the right path as teenagers.
The goal is to be there for them, make their activities and help them grow up into responsible adults.

What sacrifices if any did you make in pursuing a career? What regrets if any do you have?

Missed some of children's events.
Easier when they are younger, more difficult when they are older since they have more activities.
Forgot about school events or relied on stay at home moms to update them.
Left out time for themselves.

Left out time with women friends

Theme: While acknowledging sacrifices for their careers, participants did not express regrets.

Career, marriage, and children were all a choice for me.
You need to pursue your dreams.
Find a career you enjoy and you can have career, marriage, and children.
Work it into your life; career with marriage and children.
Sacrifices are made to yourself and to be at events of children (guilt)
Career skills are positive to decisions in the home.
Challenging and worth the effort.

APPENDIX C: INTERVIEW TRANSCRIPTS

Amber Interview

Interviewer: Give me a general outline of how you proceeded with your career. Did you plan your career?

Amber: If someone would have had a crystal ball and predicted that I would have a career. I would have never seen this as my future at all. No not at all. I always worked and it was expected and you needed a job that day and you worked grocery store, waitress, cleaned apartments. I graduated from college and was going to be pre med and then finished and I was so miserable that I did not have a social life. No plan to be a manager or even a VP. I was good at what I did and I was promoted to manager if I was a good nurse – no training, no concept of what makes a manager I just learned.

I was married at age 30 never met the right person and I wanted to take my time and the critical aspect was I would never get divorced. I wanted marriage to be forever and I wanted to take my time to make sure it was right. Was married and then started my Masters and writing a thesis 6 months later. I worked full time and Masters and married. It did not affect my relationship until I had the baby. We waited 3 years of being marriage and that was fine until we had a child. I had the baby and I worked.

Interviewer: Did it affect your relationship?

Amber: Not until we had our son. I planned the baby. Yet, I worked fulltime, never missed a day and continued on my Masters. How we get to be successful. Yet you do not see your success.

Researcher: Was your career positive or negative to marriage and children?

Amber: Career was a benefit to my life because I knew all I would ever have is me so I had to have my career. I did not trust that I would be OK without my career. I love my work. I love what I do. I never thought about balance. I never thought about not working.

I left my husband and I was not afraid, with the roles changing husband life did not change nothing was changed. I picked up more. This is the result of career role changes where women have it. You pick it up and keep on doing it. I had all the work. We have to do it all. He did do the grocery shopping. For example: things got busier he did the lawn; we paid for someone yet I had to clean the house and he continues to play and he told me I could not hire someone to clean. I can do this better myself.

Career for me was about security. When things were deteriorating in marriage he wanted another baby. I knew at that point I did not want to continue in the relationship. I wanted a partner that we can enjoy each other. It was more work than it was worth in the marriage.

Interviewer: Whom did you seek out for advice?

Amber: My supervisors were my mentors and always women. My mother said the priority is to be the best as I could and work as best as I could. Both are critical and I was provider for my child and so work was critical to be just as important or I could not support my child. Those two were my priorities as a single mom. Career was my security. And I learned that from my mother. She said security was work. My mom never yelled, never complained and did everything work, raise children and stayed married. Mom was my role model. College and work was an expectation. My mom had a college degree. She was a great role model I knew she was not happy since my parents never had a good relationship never had the caring relationship. Even if you found your prince he could be taken away at any time. My mom instilled you need to take care of yourself and survive on your own.

Interviewer: Did you think about marriage and children before your career?

Amber: No, I assumed I would be married and have children. I always worked, always would take a promotion, take on another department, never consider saying no. I can do this I did not need to talk to my husband. I can do it without a doubt no question or thoughts of anything else. As I am older, in 20-30s we as women at this level are well off financially, struggled with working mom verses career mom what was more admirable or right is my identity; it is my career. I would answer it differently now – I have achieved my accomplishments.

Interviewer: How have career choices been an opportunity or loss to marriage and child?

Amber: Career was a benefit to my life because I knew all I would ever have is me so I had to have my career. I did not trust that I would be OK without my career. I love my work. I love what I do. I never thought about balance. I never thought about not working. Yet, I felt like an anomaly to the stay at home mothers. I did not have family in town so it was important to have the support of stay at home moms. I could depend on them at a moment's notice to take my child and help me out as I was a single mom and had a career.

I left my husband and I was not afraid, with the roles changing husband life did not change nothing was changed. I picked up more. This is the result of career role changes where women have it. You pick it up and keep on doing it. It is loyalty that is important in career otherwise I will concentrate on my kid, husband and house.
As far as my child my son is at the age where he does not need me to cook. He can get his own meal and does not need me the realization means it is lonelier. Before I can do this and I can do it well. I can do it all buy my house, buy my car. My husband wa

shocked and his friends she will never walk away from the huge house and the perfect rich place. I did not have to deal with the negative. It was better for my son to put him in a less stressful situation so he would not see the discord of my marriage. And I left out me.

Interviewer: Did you have any regrets?

Amber: I had a great network of girlfriends to take care and trust them to take my child and I will be there whenever. They were stay at home moms. I was the mystery, and anomaly to them. They were more and willing to be there and be supportive and kind. Benefit to my son: responsible, resilient thought the years he makes it OK to consul me I will figure it out from my son. He is ahead of the curve. I worked harder than the men. People our age, not smarter than guys yet worked and did anything they asked us. Never said no and never left a meeting. Never would say I had to get my child.
There was a benefit to my son; he is responsible, resilient thought the years he makes it OK to consul me I will figure it out from my son. He is ahead of the curve and other things have made him independent. So there are no regrets.

Chloe Interview

Interviewer: Give me a general outline of how you proceeded with your career. Did you plan your career? Did you plan marriage and children?

Chloe: I traveled a lot and never turned down a promotion. I was director of marketing when I met my current husband. I continued to work and do the same career when I was married. What was changed as the corporate office moved to NYC and I did not move; they let me work out of my house; and I did not like working out of my home and I like and enjoy being around people and working in a office. The only thing I did not do was move around too much. I was a single mom married when child was two I was divorced. I always worked and I never thought about it. I never thought not to work. I never thought about marriage and children always assumed I would do it. People ask how you do it and you do not think about it you just do it. There is not a reflection how to accomplish it you just must get it done.

Interviewer: Was your career an opportunity or loss to marriage and children?

Chloe: I did not have a choice not to work because we wanted both incomes. When I was single mom but the company knew and so I they did not offer new positions to move, yet I still moved up the ladder yet I do believe if I would have been more open to take positions I would have moved up faster and into better positions so it was a sacrifice for my career. Yet, my daughter is the stay at home mom. I thought she would take after me and have a career. My daughter did go to daycare and my ex husband would take care of her. So I had my career and I planned to travel and handled someone to take care of her. Most women at that time were stay at home moms. I had a different life as a single mom than when someone is married. You lose friends when you divorce. The women that I was around were all related to business. I did not interface with stay at home moms. Work has changed drastically now; I believe companies are more accommodating to women and their children. If I wanted to go to a program and I could not and I never did and I never left the office I work long hard hours. Today I believe that the women are leave and go back later and do not have to work the hours we do as we were leaders in the field.

I made sure my daughter was taken care of so I could work long hours; travel; I could not take any time off in my company. As a woman, we had to work harder to be taken serious. Women cannot appear that we are not doing our job and you would never think of asking to take time off. Actually once I was established then I could work more flexible hours. While I was moving up the ladder it was creditability that was important and once it was established, it allowed you more flexibility because the company wants you to stay and knows your abilities. I never have taken on the domestic activities; cooking and cleaning. I feel like I am a nurturer, yet I did some cooking and it was easy for my daughter. The business I was in I was with the clients and I had a husband that was very social and easy to work with since he had no children. He was always supportive of me and an asset to my social events at work. There was no demanding on the domestic side. When I was a Director of training and assistant director of global programs my boss left and I did get the position. Yet for 25 years I knew what was available in the company and I was happy with promotions and happy and felt valued. I think that the grass is never greener on the other side and the position I had was very unique and I was worked up to do this job at home. My husband was not going to move out of Texas and take a job out of state. Anywhere in state was fine – now he will but not then, we could move anywhere in the state that was related to the bar.

With my first husband – I was young and married and we just grew apart. It was not about career; because I was not successful. Then it was 14 years and I was a single mom and a career woman and waiting for the right guy. When you have children you need the right guy that will gel with them and I just took awhile. I could take care of myself and I wanted to meet the right guy to marry and it took almost to 40 and being busy with a child does change your time priorities.

I married a very successful man and it was later in life I was in my late 30s and married in my 40s. I never thought not to work or to have a career or to go to college. I did not plan children it was a surprise. I have always worked and enjoyed and loved my work and never thought not to work. I love my career and enjoyed it the whole time I was there and all my experience.

Interviewer: What sacrifices or regrets do you have if any?

Chloe: Never thought of career as a sacrifice for me personally it was a wonderful great time and it was who I was and what I do. I made time for my girlfriends most were in the industry or working women. Looking back I think I was too much concentrated on my career and not enough on developing friends in town. My friends were all in the business and out of town so I wish I had developed more personal friendships than business friendships. I was with the business associates all day and I was with them and then when I was not with them I was at home. Regret only child that was not there enough for her or I missed events. And my daughter says oh mom you had to do what you had to do. Wonderful, loved it and enjoyed it. I was lucky and had a sociology degree and then I did get a business degree to help move up the ladder and then ended up getting into a great company. I never had any desire to change after I was working for Starwood hotel. I just lucked into a great career and great company.

Interviewer: Who did you seek or advice?

Chloe: My mentor was a guy who hired me and another woman that is VP at Starwood and always worked in the industry and she has always given good advice. She was in a different department than me and we always talked and she helped me in making decisions and influencing ideas. I was a sales person and an assistant director of sales position was open and a girl and I equally qualified and I went to talk to him why did you not consider me and he said you did not ask so I did not choose you. That was a good time for understanding that you needed to ask for what you wanted.

Hunter Interview

Interviewer: Give me a general outline of how you proceeded with your career. Did you plan your career?

Hunter: Husband & I met in college – he followed me to Dallas. I had my first sales job for couple of 3 years and no kids. We had a re-organization and I moved to car stereo and it was not my forte and I was traveling flying and driving and I was in bad areas. There were 3 women in division. .I was working weekends and nights and traveling and pregnant. I planned to have children after 9 years of marriage. It never entered my mind that I would not work. I worked too hard to get to that point. I won a top award while I was in the hospital having a baby. I was getting sick of position and I wanted to move up and I wanted to move up the ladder and I was making less money than the men. I could prove myself and I would stand up and stand up for myself and worked hard. I was only in a position that I did not know that I worked harder than the men.

I had great customers and I found a way the things I was good at and found a way so it worked for me. Those that followed me hated my guts because I worked hard for my clients and work for me wasn't about the money but was to be valued. One manager indicated that I would not come back after pregnancy and I was so upset and I wrote it on a piece of paper and keep it because it made me angry that they would think it. I did get a manager's position and then during that I had a second child and I had men and one older woman. I was so busy working that I pumped milk while I was in the car. I was in the van and I was breast feeding child and otherwise I would pump and put it in the refrigerator. I had a room for pumping and it is the law to provide for mothers for 6 months. On the way home from work I would pump milk on the way home. I had someone watching child.

My husband was very supportive and he was traveling more yet he was very supportive and helped with all the activities at home.

Interviewer: Did you ponder decisions on children with your career? Did you see career choices as an opportunity or loss regarding marriage and children?

Hunter: My friends that had children also worked and we all helped each other. I never asked a stay at home mom because I believed they would not think good of me and I felt guilty. My mind set was I do not want to take advantage of stay at home moms. My support system was other women that had children and careers. I was in my company for 15 years. I never thought not to work. Career was a benefit for my husband – he was not the only provider and we are allowed the opportunity to take risk – both of us could. With my second child was 3 years later and I was a manager and it took awhile to get pregnant because we were both traveling.

I was happier because I had a life outside of the home and I need it and I just had to be with adults and your kids are happy if you are happy. And when they are younger they are fine with someone to take care of them and they are in daycare and they need to be with other kids. It is a positive influence on the kids. As the children get older it is more difficult to work because then they have activities after school and you cannot be there to help them. Most my friends outside of work were all having kids and working just like me so we were together.

Interviewer: Who was your mentor or support system?

Hunter: I had no mentors – I had great bosses yet no mentors and no women working. Managers would make you feel like you could lose your job and they put on you their concerns and it was put on you to do more and work harder and sometimes fear. Loved my job and loved working and loved being a manager and I had make sacrifices because the next step up the ladder was to move and I did not want to move yet my husband was willing.

I did not have any help yet my husband and I shared in domestic and I am frugal and I can use that money for myself so for me I am wired differently than other people. My children indicates to me mom is different. Everyone was telling I need to hire some help and it drove me crazy to have everyone telling men to hire help. Yet I had great kids and they were happy and were not in trouble and my husband and I would trade off.

Then I had a new position where it was more travel and who ever traveled had to get it on the calendar first because you had to schedule and we decided who had the most important meeting would attend and the other person would have to cancel.

As a sales manager I indicated I would not travel, I had internal guilt that they would fire me if I did not do all I could to be there or to cancel anything. I made it clear that my husband and I traveled and traded off with being home for our children. My husband and I set priorities with who had the most important work event and we determined how we would juggle work with the children.

There were people that always encouraged me and not necessarily a mentor. The biggest changing point was for a manager job and I was up against a man that had been in the industry for more years than me and my boss encouraged me and I had to decide what can I offer that was different with a person that has more experience in this company than me – what do I have to offer. And I did get the job and I do not like to brag and they did hire me and it was someone I did not know and I researched and I did give them reasons. Made me feel good to know I can do this.

Interviewer: Did you see career as an opportunity or loss to your children?

Hunter: It was easier when I was manager because I did not have to travel as much then as when I was a sales person. As a sales manager you are out in the thick of it. As a manager you do work longer hours because of different hours around the USA so you were the first and the last to leave. I was able to be an account manager in the military and the manager and after two days he quit and I ended up with his job. Then the office moved farther away and I was feeling guilty and my husband was traveling and I did have a choice. I like work and I like to be busy and I like to move up and I liked to talk to directors anytime I wanted to and I was important. My management style I was too much hands on; I had done all the jobs that my sales force did so I knew the tools that had and what was necessary to make their job successful. I had to fire a person and I had accounts calling me and I was fair for everybody and I understood it is demeaning to you if you cannot win a sales award if I was not fair and I always fought for my staff. And my staff did get used to doing things for them all the time. I enjoyed yet I ended up needing to move to make the next step to be a VP.

Interview: What regrets or sacrifices did you have to make if any?

Hunter: My only regret there was times that I could have chosen a path and I needed to have good clients to have a personal repertoire and relationship with my clients and with those that worked for me. I was the hard worker I believe in the work ethic and I believe you have to work hard and I will do it at every level yet those that are hard workers - hard work men or women and you can succeed and you can do it and many that worked for me are successful today.

People usually came to me with the promotions and I stayed and worked with the company because they knew me. I was getting job offers all the time yet I never thought to leave my company. I worked for the best company and I am valued and I respected the company and we are the best. That is what made me able to do it and I liked it so much and liked the people and if I left it would be in a total different field. As the children get older and they have after school that is most difficult. They do not need you when they are younger.

I never thought I would get where I am today and have a successful career and move up in the company. I was lucky to be given the opportunities and I never planned the career just planned to work and work hard and have values and ethics.

Interviewer: Any advice to younger women?

Hunter: I would tell them to find a career where they can work flexible hours so they could have both marriage and children and work. Yet, make sure they find the job they love where they can have it all and be able to work their career with their children.

Jasmine Interview

Interviewer: Give me a general background of your career and the decisions you made?

Jasmine: It was the 1970s and companies needed to have a woman in sales, I learned all tech talk, industry, mainly I can sell and I had a product and 2 years later Dallas had to hire minorities (1974). I was married at 23 and miscarried twice. I was divorced because the husband was nice but an underachiever. He just did not have the same motivation to succeed as I did. I became the sales manager, put me in the board room then hired a black man and door in room said token room. He received more money than me because he was a man and they told me he did. I was to train him. Supervisor or boss leave (even men) and they would put her in position because next qualified person, although they said it was temporary until they hired someone. Yet, I learned the job because I was doing it and doing it so well they left me and that is how I ended up with positions. I worked 12-14 hour days. I was the first women Director of Bureau in USA. There was a first woman in hotels was a friend; and we were the two first women in our industry. Men treated you as a sex object. Men would touch my breast and I would say it loudly I am sorry my breast interfered with your hand so others would hear and be embarrassments. They call me by a man name because men were not used to dealing with women. I set the boundaries with the men. I liked all my jobs yet liked management best. Men were rude at that time in board meetings such as reading paper when I was conducting meeting and I had to be forceful and direct the room. I was great friends after because I was good and I worked hard the 12-14 hour days, nights and weekends.

Interviewer: Was your career an opportunity or loss to marriage and children?

Jasmine: In the late 70s I met my husband in the industry in another city. This was the first time to date someone in the industry and we kept it quiet and no one knew because he was a 20 years older. Finally after a couple of years told my boss and they said fine unless we were in the same city. When he moved to Dallas I had to resign after we were married because I was married and I could not get a job. I could not get a job for two years yet I did consulting because knew me and I would get work and was full time as a consultant. Freedman bought my husband's company and then since my husband sold then I could work. You could not relate so I worked freelance for the company for 27 years full time position. Second time married 34 years old and her husband sold to Greyhound Bus Company. Day we moved in house in Las Vegas; I want to buy you out and I want your husband and me to run the company because we know the business. Then moved back to Dallas and joined Freedman. Then we were able to work together. My husband was the smartest man I know. We had the best marriage and later worked together and traveled together. I was in the convention business and hotel centers.

I had 30 seconds of thought about a child with my husband and decided no; I have 3 stepchildren, I never was interested in children, they scare me and I never worried about it again. My husband had 3 children from a previous marriage and the youngest child was around 13 so she is the one I am closest to today. Yes, I did try to do it all. I was the one to cook, do laundry, arrange for step children, pick them up. I did hire someone to clean the house. Yet the other domestic chores I took on myself, I just did them. I did not feel a loss of career from marriage and or children. I wanted to be independent and then figure out what I want to do and thought maybe I was not capable of love, it just wasn't for me.

Never found it a loss; I know I am strange and different; but I never saw it as a loss or had any regrets. I was close friends with men yet I respected the boundaries, never knew the wives. I had very few women friends. I was always with men, weeks on the road. As I was older and joined the bureau yet they did not want to be involved with me. I was an island. I did not have any girlfriends that were home married with children. I made them uncomfortable I was the one that traveled with their husbands. I am very independent and I liked my own self and my own company. I make other women uncomfortable. I want women friends and I want them to be strong and independent and I do not like whining. I did not want to hear about women complaining not doing something with their lives.

Interviewer: Did you make a choice in your career.

Jasmine: I did not have a choice in working or never thought of it as a choice. I worked and after husband died work was not fun anymore because we traveled together and worked together it was fun. Prior to meeting husband I pursued my job and men were intimated by a woman that worked in a high level position and did not want to date me. I am having a difficult time not working it is what I do. I resigned the last year before he died and said it was not my passion anymore and it is your passion. After I made the decision he became sick. I resigned and had a big party and left and felt a relief with my briefcase and back to hotel and felt I was walking out of cave into the light. Because I had done this for 33 years and I wanted to find another passion another direction.

I was a workaholic and I married a man that was a workaholic and I married later in my mid 30s prior to that time I was working and devoted to work and did not think of relationship or children as a priority. We worked together and married together so we could combine working and fun.

I left my job and I had no business card no job no business card and I was drinking Dom and I was in Hawaii in a suite and I started crying and I have no job and I was afraid, I was eye candy for my husband and that was late in life.

Interviewer: Who was your mentor or you support system?

Jasmine: I had no mentors. There were not any other women in the industry. And I could not have a man as a mentor. I learned on my own by myself. I do believe we marry the male version of who we would be if we were a man and I believe men marry what the female version of the person they would be if they were a woman. He was smart and had wisdom and I was good for him because I could communicate and I was social and I could handle any situation. He was so high up in the company that he was alone and he was quiet.

The people I admire were independent people. Even women I know that are married and have children are independent and work and have strong characters. Women look for someone to take care of them. I thought it was nice when I married my husband that it was nice he had money, yet I had money too.

I struggle with balance, I worked, I took care of the step children, I packed when I moved, and I did not know what not to do. I was an enabler.

Interviewer: Did you ponder decisions and changes in the future?

Jasmine: I just have to do it all! Yes it was what I did and I knew no different. I worked when my husband was sick and I ran his company so he received a salary and I had to travel run the company and by then I had the credibility and I wanted him to keep his power as long as he could. People were used to me and I never went away and I ran the company. After he passed away they hired me to do stuff for 2 years to run his company. I need to find out what I want to do; because I want to live a great life and I need to have a job and live the life I do. Husband left me comfortable and he had some to his children. My goal work to bring income; humanitarian to give back (women for women) children scare me give me a boardroom and I am fine give me a 2 year old and I will be on my knees not knowing what to do. My stepchild a love/hate thing because she loved me, step son that committed suicide and oldest stepchild did not have children. None of my friends have children. So the children stuff is scary.

Interviewer: What advice would you give to younger women?

Balance is the most important, work became my life and it was the most important thing and I did not balance my personal identity, my husband married a woman that had a title a powerful woman and that is what I offered my husband. As a widower I now think: What can I offer a husband when I did something yet he did not see me walk that path? You need to balance early on because I was strange I worked I never knew to do anything else. Today hopefully women are at a place when they can have it all they can balance by knowing who they are in the beginning to have your own self worth and then know you're good and bad so you can work it into your life and work into your schedule so you have marriage and children with your career. Now a days they did not have to fight to be a woman they have that this new generation it is working 8-5 and get it done, I worked until 8 or 9pm working 14 hour day and Sundays were normal. Women today can do it all and they are equal, we did that so hopefully we paved the way for them so they are equal for most part and now can have it all and balance work with marriage and/or children. I could not have been a wife or mother; I am a great aunt, step mother etc as long as they are 10 or older. I have the nurturer as long as I had work first. I just did not think about it. I never turned down a promotion, worked hard to move up the ladder and never contemplated whether it was the right thing to do.

Kayla Interview

Interviewer: Can you give me a general outline of how you proceeded with your career?

Kayla: I worked for TV station, post production then saw advertising companies and said I know more than them and they did get free lunches and ended up as director at Tracey Locke advertising agency then they merged with DB to get McDonalds. Then I became executive producer with DB and then I did most of the fun part of my career and anything that was done there was 10 -15 projects – TV, radio, events, great jobs, great opportunity and loved my job and then I had a child and when I left I decided to go with another company.

Interviewer: Did you consider marriage and children during your career?

Kayla: I was married and he was married before and I did want to have children and could not and first husband was a career idiot and we were married 11 years. I was 36 when I met my current husband and he was in the middle of the divorce and I was pregnant and we got married after she was 18 months. I was working and my current husband and I wanted children and did not have children and I worked as many hours as I wanted to and I worked as much as I wanted and I worked long hours and weekends and my husband had no problem.

When I had a baby I was at Tracy Locke and I worked for 5 years. I was having fun and I was producing and working and I really loved producing. I always was happy and I wished I could do other things. I am a control freak and I loved to do what I did. I had the option to leave since he was making more than both of us. And we had to balance custody of his daughter at teenage and so I had his daughter and our daughter. It has not been easy blended families and with CEO executive husbands and me me me- take care of me and my day.

I had a nanny, I had someone to help out and I never wanted to leave my job yet I thought I was selfish for my child and then with the blended family I had a step daughter. I wish I could put her in a nursery and we went through 5 nannies before I could decide this is not working and I needed to stay home.

They did not allow you to work at home or to work part time –I tried through my company and I could do my job at home, yet they refused I had to work full time in the office or not have a job. Yet, they were running commercials on the work at home the new internet technology and maybe this will change with the next generation.
I had all men at that time that I was working for and with and that was the story. It was OK and I was ready to move on and deal with the next phase and be home for 8 months and he indicated to me you are ready to move on and I was never so miserable in my life and there was nothing for me and I did not make the transition very well and I had to go back to work and I learned so many new things and worked with my husband. I could not be at home and he understood I need to be happy and he loves me and so I was working for him for 4 years and then he closed his company and then I never knew what to do and then I decided ok I will do my own thing. I was only paid if I did what I said I would do and I was representing those in broadcasting company. Yet I had so many people, yet I was not happy I was making 16 phone calls and I found out that I was not doing what I was happy and I was screening production and this is what you hire. You have your own agency and then the light bulb went off and I knew I had the best people Motel 6, Starbucks and all these amazing creative's from my history of advertising to support me. I do not have time for too many and I am going after big ones and I am a producer yet print and media I did not know as much about. I had one client as a training wheel.

Interviewer: What regrets or sacrifices did you have if any?

We are the nurturers; I have to be there for my kids. That is the struggle for all executive women we have to sacrifice the career or the husband or the children and I had a screwed up child and I would have another child along and I have sacrificed while staying at home and I would rather work and there is so many women that they are working and they do not have a child – work is easy children are difficult, younger is easier and teenagers are more difficult yet you have to bake the cake and watch the temperature and make sure you do all. I am doing more and I am juggling and I work all night yet I left to do my own company and I can only work half a work week until younger daughter drives.

Men are attracted to successful women. On my street, all were executive women one for Neiman Marcus buyer, one a doctor that all quit to be a stay at home mom.
My neighbors and close friends are doing something; they at least work part time or they help their husband or do something to do to keep in the business.

You have to make choices and you have to make choices and decide what to do with the cdren. I would take a baby with me in meetings and with week end editorials I was working and I was the top person I did not ask I just did it and I was in charge of the production and I would take my child with me. I would not take her with me when I traveled and my husband would take care of her. I was in charge of everything.

Interviewer: What advice would you give younger women?

Kayla: We as women at our age always worked with women and were in control and strong and today women are the same because men have not changed.
Today I see more women that have the money and they make the money and their husband is at home more they have a man that works yet will stay at home more. Women have more degrees and have more experience and have more education and work experience. Women and men are different we are wired differently.

Women's movement is great yet it is such a burden and we have had to make sacrifices and we have live up to the movement. My time will come when my child is in college and I have two wonderful girls and a happy marriage and it is wonderful and I am, very lucky and I have no regrets I have made sacrifices and I have no regrets and I have so much to be thankful for.

I just do it, and we just do it and that is it. My mother says slow down and I am just high energy and high activity and it is difficult to ever do so. Yet I have to do something for me for my self esteem and in 2 years when my last child is 18 then it is a time for me to pursue my goals and my game to the maximum. This is my opportunity to be the best I can be at every stage of the game...

Megan Interview

Interviewer: Give me a general outline of how you proceeded with your career. Did you plan your career?

Megan: I have a college degree; international and business degree which is the perfect blend of analytical and relationship business. Yet, college is difficult and you do not know what you want to do ...you are clueless...you can tell the kids that have been coached and those that have not been in business world and I do not know how to not work.

I was fortunate to have a mentor. My Dad was influential to my career – needed the shove to push me over. My parents were college educated. My mom said you cannot be a nurse because you cannot be subservient. I had strong parents. I started out in training program and my boyfriend now husband did not want to move to Houston so compromise was Dallas he wanted to be in Austin. My husband was a very traditional family and it was not appropriate to have mom work. My dad was fine whatever my mom did.

My husband tells me "he loves me in spite of your job". He does not care where I work. The balance of powers is important. It is important to me for both of us to have an equal stake in financial. In the last 10 years I made more money. I was careful that he was He said I do not need to work – I said you need to work. I like the balance of power. I am in a male dominated industry. Only one other woman in role and it was in private banking so I did not want to go into female area. I have a male mentor that was my boss. I have to be here yet I am at the level of being able to do my own thing. I have the presence because of the level I am at.

Interviewer: What choices did you make in your career for marriage and children?

Megan: The work for me is easier when they are older, yet I have good kids. I have had nannies and I had a stay a home mom that we paid and she was my neighbor and she also cooked. My husband and I balance with the kids. My 2nd son was born, I lost my father and we had a difficult time. I had to ask my husband to help and to do things. Instead of talking about it I just was madder and I was more aggressive and he becomes more passive aggressive and we had to figure it out. I felt like he was helping me out with the kids, yet I never vocalized.

Never planned career, or children – never a question, I just thought I would figure it out. First kid I was not a manager, with the 2nd kid I was a manager and moved up to supervisor and I had to go through the mindset am I prepared to derail my career for my family. Yet, I did go to my boss and I said I will take a 20% cut in salary and work 4 days – worked 10-12 hours a day and it was worth it yet I was getting more done and I was at story hour. Yet then I was promoted and it was with my mentor and he knew I could do this. My boss promoted me as he was promoted. I tell young women to be the best you can be in the job that you are in – we have a open culture to promote within the company and all the people had a hand in their success. I had one person that mentored me. I did go to him and said I love what I do but I am bored. I had a call to run the trust department and it was a big stepping stone I managed over 80 people in 4 locations and had to fire people and I had both kids. Then I ran this department until I was ready for a new challenge. I did go to higher level job and I said here is what I want to do. And he said move and I said no and he said it is OK and then you are out of the roles and you have to move. So then I decided I did not want to move and I want to stay in this city and you better talk to her before she leaves and she is the one for this job.

Husband should be equal in the home to help out. We as women and men have traditional roles – in the house my mom used to run the house yet I am not around to do that so he has to help out. Traditional values are important, yet my mom ran the house and we reported to my mom" and I cannot do that I cannot run the house alone.

Career is as benefit to my husband. Career is a benefit for my children. It is a benefit. They may not realize it but it is a benefit. I had a presentation on work/family balance so I did research. So I explained concept a 1 – 10 (10 is a 100) what grade to you give me. My older son said I give you a 70 on that is average. That is a C – what would make me get a 90 or 100. I was braced for the guilt trip. "He said Mom you talk to me like I work for you and if you did not use all these work words and you did treat me like I work for you then you would be a 90. Average is not acceptable for a driven type A personality. I said what can I do? – if you would not treat me like an employee "thank you for the feedback" and he said that is my point – you treat me like an employee you just did it see that is one of those words. My 2nd son said I give you an 80 and what can I do to get 90 and he said "I would like you around".

Children see work comes first yet. I want them to know they come first and I started having breakfast with my children on Fridays until my one son said sleep is more important than breakfast. I am trying to be there more for them and make them know they are first. I can work 24 hours a day with a computer and cell phone – in our day we could not do that. Hopefully my kids will not know that it is traditional for women to cook at home they like to cook and they are boys. My son said I am going through a process that I was gone more nights and I am gone at least 2 nights. My son told me, "I do not take time for myself; accept for running and Yoga on Saturday"
.

My women friends, I have not cultivated friends if we are not doing something for work then I would rather be home and relax. I like type A types and I do not look down on stay at home moms – I think I am intimating to them. I have more in common with the ones working – "you are so smart and I cannot keep up with it" stay at home mom.
It is hard for them to be around me as they are difficult with me. I drifted over to the guys because "I understand them better and have more in common with them". I live in the moment – I do think about future I cannot imagine not working. My husband would be ready for me to slow down I see another crisis coming in the future…I cannot see myself not working. I think it is funny I have a women like me that works in Michigan and there are only two bankers that are women, I look at Midwest as progressive, yet something is missing.

Interviewer: What advice would you give to young women?

Megan: I try to be very realistic – 50% of the women are able to contain in the business at the professional level. At the professional level they have to work the hours and be in the office. I think the next generation if you get through the first 10 years at work and you have kids older then you can wait and it will be easier. My husband moved his office home after 5-6 nannies and mental breakdown and stressed and he moved home and took on 20% less clients. It is important to just work things out and handle and prioritize.

Nora Interview

Interviewer: Can you give a general outline of your career. Did you plan your career?

Nora: I always worked out of 28 years of married life; I have worked 26 ½ because of different timing. I worked through college and I did get a degree in home economics – knew I did not want to teach – both of my parents had college degrees. I attended Texas Tech and satisfied both parents. I have the work ethic. There was no decision, no choice to do anything yet go to college – worked part-time in college for a career oriented woman and then after college they hired me. After she left, a new man took her place and I did not want to work for took over position so I started looking to leave.

Interviewer: Whom did you seek for advice as a mentor or support?

Nora: My women mentor helped find a new job for me because she said I know someone you should talk to and started working in a sales role Research corporation of American selling tax and legal information to sell to attorneys and ended up #1 in company, then number 2 and it was a natural fit and I traveled while single throughout the southwest. Then I met my husband; he is military trained and based in his career. So I did have to move for marriage and I had to move for his new assignments. I was planning to move to Austin and needed to move 4-5 months early and I had huge bonuses; he said fine yet did not keep his promise and hired a man for the job. I was the 5th woman hired and the youngest person; I only called on 3 women; every partner or every law firm and every CPA firm were men. My mentors were men after the first woman. The 2nd manager was my most significant mentor and very key in my life.

Women were their own worst enemies women wanted to work for men and had a problem working with women and there was no mentoring. My woman mentor had the view you can do what you want to do and she commanded respect from men and she was a take charge woman and that is what I did too. I was an outside sales rep and had to work independently and it is your results and numbers that tell your story on what you did – I just went out and take it. I only would see my manager once a month and then once a quarter – it was based on numbers and a phone call to find out how you did.

Interviewer: How have career choices been an opportunity or loss regarding marriage and children?

Nora: The first change of job was demanded because of getting married and while manager did not have a territory in Austin and then I took another and it was a Dallas territory and work that with a husband and a new house and work in Dallas all week and then arrive Friday at 8pm and nothing was done to put the house together.

I never considered not working – probably a good idea – yet I was programmed that way and I was the top person and I have an income level at a stage I really loved and can live this lifestyle. I usually dated older men that were successful and ok with a strong independent woman. Yet my husband was the same age is me and he was ok with my independence. Men are intimated by strong women. Women cannot change they are who they are who I am today; my daughter doesn't date and she is very strong and very driven and is not the dating kind.

I never have ridden down goals, I never planned. Sales fit my personality and I was competitive and driven to do the absolute best. Sales were a normal and natural career for me.

In an interview for pharmaceutical sales I was asked; where do you see yourself in 10 years and I said having a happy family. So there was a desire to have a family unit that was functional. I worked up to the day I had the baby and did not want children to have until after 30 and I let God make the choice for me and I was pregnant and I was ok with it there is a lot of challenges with kids and I have grown more in that area and yet they have not turned out exactly like I wanted yet you do not get to pick your kids it is not a utopia. At lot of my friends do have time passage and then decide later if they want a child. Having a child is the desire to nurture. I never had a strong need for nurturing – it was strong in faith and I am, programmed a certain way.

I had a nanny and I have a boy and a girl. In a sales role I did not want to have kids because I could make more money. Sales manager was a benefit because I could have a steady salary and I could move in the ladder. Yet in sales you can make more money in sales than in management. I had my first child 8 years later. I had more flexibility as a sales manager and I had 9 men and 1 woman reporting to me and you just do what you have to do and I was pregnant during that time.

I am sure I felt short in different areas yet is a good balance and we made it work. My husband was based in Dallas and we lived in Atlanta and I had a full time person living with me. And I could work the hours I wanted to work.

I had minimum contact with stay at home moms. I had a neighbor stay at home mom and they liked to be at my house. The kids were instrumental meeting the parents and I hired the mom to be my assistant. When you spend time with another woman you have common paths and common interests. Stay at home mom takes more time and effort. Most of the stays at home moms were from my church. I moved to Atlanta and I choose that church because they did not ask me how many kids I had and they had kids and I didn't and most in my age bracket started early. Most of the stay at home moms through church was there when I had my baby and helped because my husband was not home. We lived in different cities.

I absolutely enjoy work and I enjoy people. I justified that I have been given the skills and gift and the passion to be given the skills to work and not question that I could do both and I had great people to help. There is the feeling that if I had stayed at home with my son that he would have been different yet there are stay at home moms where they have children in trouble – it happens.

Interviewer: What advice would you give to younger women?

Nora: I would be interested to ask my daughter would you have liked your mom to do it differently. Do they see it differently? I do believe we each have to work it out for ourselves. I did reach a point of frustration at my corporation with their management style and did decide then give to my children and give to my other responsibilities. Yet my company rode me consistently and it became a very bad situation – I hated it with a passion yet, I did not want to give up the money I was making so much money. I knew I could be the best yet I had dropped down a few levels. My old men peers hate their job yet are so tied to the money and then I made a break and I was 6 figures consistently and I just left and I have a new position. I made a great change to be valued. I did not feel valued – I was devalued – the company made me feel I was devalued and that was why I left and went with another company it was never an issue of my family. I hated the corporation to the degree that I throw in the towel for the interest in being married because my husband that does not like the inconvenience since we lived in different cities and he wanted it convenient for him.

My husband and I traveled about the same amount; yet, my husband had to commute to his job. I was in Atlanta he worked in Dallas and my company found a job in Oklahoma. It was a mutual compromise. I was a sales manager and then a director of sales both roles where I traveled yet the easiest position for me was as a sales manager; I could direct and guide people. I left because I did not like the direction the company was taking and the way they devalued me so that day was what are you bringing in today for sales and what are your numbers and what are your results.

Ruby Interview

Interviewer: Can you give a general outline of how you proceeded with your career and the decisions you made in the process regarding marriage and children?

Ruby: I am a corporate executive in the health care industry. Business marketing moved to New York and started pharmaceutical company. 6 years with genetic – the company was worth 28 to 100 million dollars. I was the only woman and built the company. Next I made a name in the diabetic consumer market 2 ½ years – always traveling – I love to travel, modify my life – like family and roots and love traveling. I was also in Biocraft – Trammel Crow; public companies. Japanese company- does not respect women. I proved my way with them – they consolidated, I just found opportunities, Healthcare division fI was the only woman. At first being a woman I have no fear. Promoted ran national contacts moved to Dallas in 1988 Impact in 1989 commute Dallas to California.

I was 31 and decided to get married to have kids. We were married to have children. DO it all. I started my deal in 91 and we had our first daughter all retail and I built it to 800 million (then had second child) sold company for 3.5 billion dollars. I was going to take a break did not happen – let me ride my ride. And why would I not want to do it and I made a lot of money and why would I not want to do it. I worked for a Fortune 500 company, nanny, lady that kept kids in home. I moved them to day care. Husband helped, but when I was home it is your turn – work together to get it done – he never traveled and I was working. He wanted to have his guy time there was no US time and now he is my best friend.

Great run with Fox and affiliates for 4 years and I ran everything and I was the only women except for CFO was a woman. No mentors. I had great bosses all the bosses. Working together for 5 years we made decisions in the board room and never left until we were done – photos to our spouses for Christmas because we did not see them. You become one of the guys. My boss asked me when I made the choice to go to Fox for my feedback. I decided to leave and move to Ohio and I was not going to leave with 2 kids same dad married to him twice – now he is a good dad. Kids weather all the storms. I did understand but I was the only female in the executive team – I felt like I put more emotional energy in it and he wanted new blood and acquire Fox and put me in the position to wake people up the good old boy network. It is emotional and you have to hold back and they do not get it like we do. We compensate to fit in their world. It is difficult to shut it off. You go you are accustomed to doing it and I just do it I get up at 6am and I do the same thing and I make sure everyone is doing what they have to do it is not that hard. It is timing all is about timing. You just do it and it is part of my esteem no way that I will not have a career.

When I resigned from Impact we were close and he did an exit interview and it was amazing because he asked me advice on a boss. He was willing to ask me and ran a wonderful team and he pursued me for the job and she said the problem is that he tried to mold me into him and the mindset of doing things a certain way. You can guide us and manage us and then how we get there is up to us. It doesn't work for me, there are people that like to control so if it works for them then that is the way you have to do it. They buy and want me to do business because they want me and what is unique to me and I want to do things my way. We fit into their man world. Cram the square peg into the round hole. I do believe adversity is going to be the challenge to the next generation – lots out of their control to affect where they are going to go and will the opportunities be there to take on. I talk to my kids and they have to know the truth about life it is not easy they see the pain and agony what does it take to get these things.

I think small children are fine and it is only when they are teenagers that they need you and I had some problems with my older child. Then they need the mother if they are girls and they need father if they are sons. I acquire pharmacy Automation Company –

prescription pharmacy and automation was the buzz world. Ended up buying the company and I did that and I was approached by CEO and he pursued me for the position. They offered me an opportunity (Fortune 50 company with a ton of stock and I was going to leave to be more creative). I can make money again, I took the start up job because I wanted to do it on my own and be creative we bought 6 companies and in 3 years sold the company and I commuted to Pittsburgh sales and services, they hired me after they bought this company. My oldest having issues and she was going the wrong direction and I said I need to think about it because I was divorced yet I had a nanny that was part of my family. 2003 decided to leave; I wanted to start a company; the value of relationships, business and I wanted to started my own company. It did not work did not want me to leave – stock and money at me; this is about my kids I have been giving and giving to corporate America for 20 years and I need to give to my children. Boss wanted to find a place for me and I wanted to leave to be with my kids and he said ok and he said stay through the end and we will let you choose what you want to do. I will commit 2 year contract and we will be your first client – stock etc. it was a relief; I was home on a regular basis 2004 started my company I had to hire people so I can help at home and then my child had problems and my brother died. God works in mystery ways and allow me to deal with all of this and I could not have done this is corporate America.
It all worked out and my kids are good and working and we have a balance in our household and in our life and I travel yet I choose what I do and where I go and I have a startup of an opportunity. You have to have foresight and things click – I never asked for anything, never for a promotion or a step up just worked hard and this is what I do and have to do - it is for me.

Interviewer: How has career been an opportunity or loss regarding marriage and children?

Ruby: It is a chest of drawers; each drawer – career, personal, children and we multi task and men compartmentalize; my strengths are cross structure I just go and know what I going to do and always work. I do balance my time; friends, network and charity and church. A book that tells it all is the "Power of Who" – how utilizing your networks – who do you know who do you call on who do you network with – there is adversity and it is a time for reflection what works and doesn't work and how to deal. My parents are so happy and have been together forever. Non e of my family is here and nanny and friends are part of the network to make it happen. Ex husband stays with kids and my older kids pick up their responsibilities to pick up the slack and do what they have to do they are so conscientious I was 38 years old with my first and you just handle and do it and the kids know that they need to do things.

Ex and I put our children first; we were married twice and I love him yet I am not in love; we are too different – he is anti social – I think my career affected his ability to deal with the relationship since I was doing so well and he was not in control and he took a backseat to me. And I divorced him because he started going out and doing things that were not right. He was out at night when the kids were home. I helped him by divorcing him because he changed his life. I will tell you we would socialize in groups and we did not have as much one on one time that we needed yet he blamed me for his inability to succeed – I had resentment – I tell you something I am going to do it and he did get in trouble and he had to fall down to deal with it – I was not his mother I was his wife. No I let him fall. I hit a wall and would see if he would adapt – I said he is the one that has to deal with his behavior and I sat out. I have enough stress without worrying house is tumbling down and my kids are not going to suffer. We are great friends and we are there for the kids. Why fix what is not broken I am content and I love my ex yet I do not want to fix it I want it to work now. Determine who you can live with and who you can live without. I have him there for the kids and I have a lot of guy friends and I want to enjoy my life and I do not want to have someone in my life. If a relationship is too much work it is not worth it.

Interviewer: What advice would you give to younger women?

Ruby: The next generation will not be as successful as us. They will have less and do less and have fewer opportunities. They will deal with adversity and challenges and will have a difficult time realizing they will not provide for their children like we did for our children.

Sophie Interview

Interviewer: Can you give a general outline of how you proceeded with your career and the decisions you made in choices of marriage and children?

Sophie: I have a graphic design degree and it is design; color, structure, visual implementation; how design and concepts relate to anything. This relates to resumes I read, if they are nicely laid out then the person has attention to detail, professional appropriate and these skills translates to their work. I moved to Dallas to get job. I worked the way through school as a waitress – 15 jobs great work ethic. Family – dad supported, mom worked part time lesson be responsible and be there for your children and be ethical. I was in a top furniture creative division; learned a lot most from this company; manager left and I took over and had no experience in management. I worked with vendors visited people from all over the country. One year and then I was a manager – that job taught me enough that I wanted to manage people; multitasking, controlling and I knew I these were my skill sets.

Through personality tests I am told I am direct; control no nonsense deal with reality and practically more than the emotions. As far as learning it taught me about business and working with people and managing people. I like doing it all and I was creative get mattresses and I was hauling chairs in freight elevators and this woman would watch me work and finally she came over to me and said I do not know what you do but you work so hard and I do not know what you do yet I have a friend that needs someone in retail. I started working as assistant manager one year and then my manager left and for 7 months

I worked as manager – of course I thought I could do it yet I was young and it was a flagship store and I did not have the experience of those much older than me.

There were some changes in my ideas at the beginning when I was engaged. My current company was very successful yet, I had a friend that was an art teacher and since I was not going to get the manager job and I was engaged I could get back to creative as art teacher; did get my teaching degree and masters in art while I was married. In 2 years and was working back in the business world. I was a teacher for awhile and they hired me and said I can teach art while finishing school. I did it for 2 years yet I did it in 3 years; newly married and became teacher worked with high school students and there was trouble; razor blades, drugs and I felt like their friend than a teacher or authoritarian. What I learned from teaching; I was happy teaching and someone called me that had been promoted and she wanted me back. I had women that I reported to were great examples and mentors and shaped me and my career and having those examples.

Interviewer: During that time who did you seek for advice; any mentors or support system?

Sophie: I grew up having lots of girl friends yet I enjoy hanging out with the guys and they were my friends. I prefer working with women as boss. I agree to take job; I interviewed and got the job; after 6 months we had top floor; it was a higher paying position and I took the job. It was great business was successful, what I brought with it was the softer version of the woman boss (she was a health nut, great with numbers) I found the commission sales people never talked to each other and developed a team and used my creative art side and my people side and gave them a reason to come together which they never had before and I thought it was interested that is impacted them and a relationship with us; I see them still – women reaching out to women. My boss moved on to another company. She said she was not leaving unless I go and I worshipped her and knew she was working for my best interest. I was afraid to job hop and I always trusted her and she was always loyal and looking out for me. So I decided to interview and I liked it and knew I could grow the business and it seemed like a good thing and I was offered the position and accepted it and of course she accepted it too. She interviewed for the high end jewelry retail company job and told me about it; all was well yet there were changes that were going and she realized conflicts were arising and I knew my boss was going to leave. I felt I should leave or watch for opportunities.

She took another job not the one she interviewed for at high end jewelry retail and she met with my current boss and they had dinner told her about the sales manager position yet salary was too low for her and her experience and so she told the interviewee I have a little gift for you and I have her resume and yet I never applied for a job. People just recommended me and as a mentor they moved me along. I interviewed with a woman who was my mentor and said if they do not hire you I am going to steal your ideas. It has been 10 years with the same company. I started as sales manager and am director. As sales manager I realized working with high school students was exactly like working with the people at the store just the same just different size people. It was the same or similar as teaching. Then we opened another store planned my pregnancy and first time I was pregnant; I was so comfortable at this place and knew I would stay and my friends were having children and it seemed like the right time. I worked to end and then had baby came back worked 3 years had another child and did the same thing. I changed my hours and my routine. My husband travels all the time and he was gone Monday through Thursday so I had a lot of responsibility here – yet I felt like a single mom and we were open on the week end. Every week my husband was the dad on duty I had Friday as my day off and Sunday we alternate. I had a babysitter for 6 years.

Interviewer: Did you have any regrets or feelings of sacrifice to your marriage or children?

Sophie: Yes, when they were younger they did not know and as long as they were taken care of it was fine. As they get older it is more difficult. They did call me mom and would be with me even with the nanny. I would get home at 6 or 7 at night so our time was quality time; laundry, dishes done all of our time was playing and talking except my days off. We had our time to do fun things. I think that is what created our strong bond. Now children want me to be there for all activities; she wants me to come and be at lunch concert – I have to pick and choose due to my work. There are times when I cannot do things like that and she has cried and the majority of the moms don't work – so that is what she sees moms at school all the time. Other moms will take them, yet I have someone to take care of them and choosing right person is important. And nanny needs to help with homework and do things that are more challenging. Girls started school they need to have help and I can only check and go over; I need their homework done. I sometimes get home at 8pm at night.

Interviewer: How have career choices been an opportunity or loss to marriage and children?

Sophie: Overall, I hear different philosophies, I think I am setting a good example for my girls whatever level they take it serious realize it is a project their minds are forming and they take responsibility for their actions and they see they need to be responsible and complete tasks.

As far as my husband, he is fun and more free going even though he has a serious career. He is his own business owner. I feel like I have more responsibilities and bring work home. I am the more structured than him he is the fun enjoying have a good time. I am more stressed and I have to take more work home.

We have a great balance. Before kids was more challenging because it was the kids that forced us to be together. We are both career driven and as soon as we had kids we need to be home more and change our priorities. My husband is there doing what I need – his job allows for flexibility. He is the type of person that is so willing and he stayed home and watched the kids on weekends for many years. In general I do work weekends because it is best for the business. He knows they are his children as mine. He will cook, play with the kids and focus on what needs to get done. When he is home he cooks and when not nanny does it. I struggled for a long time that I wanted to be there for dinner. I get the up extra early so we can have breakfast together. I have all organized the night before. Women are wired differently. I have learned the last several years that I have to say no to my family and friends not my work, prior to that I said yes to friends and family. I work so hard I need to say no to my family and friends so we can have our own Christmas and events.

Interviewer: Who do you seek out for advice as mentors or your support system?

Sophie: The mentors I have made it easy to move up the ladder. I do not think I cannot work – I look at friends and family that do not work I can imagine it I do not know something is in me I have to work I feel the need to work I thought about it when I had the children. I choose not to stay home; couple of different reasons – reason I did not want to work part time is because of financial yet the answer was no it is part of me controlling.

Interviewer: Did you think about decisions in marriage and children before embarking on your career?

Sophie: I never planned it – I thought I want to be a teacher or graphic designer. I worked my way up and it was all about serving people – guide them and provide functions for them. Give them some different themes and authority where people ask you for advice how to gain customers and built relationships and it is my strength and it comes out. I am not looking for the next promotion it has just come up. Every promotion I have though do I want to take the extra promotion, yet my mentor helped me and I could not turn down the job. I found them generous and I was fortunate to get the promotion and have someone who is my boss let me decide where I would work.

My time was divided by work and two children far different from work and one child yet working and making more money allowed me to provide more for them to give more for their education. And when I thought about not taking the promotion I knew it could be me and I was good and I did not want to report to another person. I knew the position and could do the job and did not want to give that up.

Having the ability to make decisions and do what is right for the store and I can do it. Worked hard good at what I did and enjoy it.

Interviewer: What advice would you give for younger women?

Sophie: To find what makes you happy and work towards that and not to wait or someone will provide for me and to be independent and not to rely on someone to be financial or emotionally dependent. Do what drives you and work hard and if you have an opportunity to stay home fine yet I have chosen a different time. Some kids cling to their mothers and takes time to take to the school they are crying because they are so upset mine are used to me getting up and leaving and I will put them in the hands of someone I trust and I think the example I am setting for the girls is the right one. And my children are young yet in the future they will be in college and gone and what would I do entering a career later after I leave it because it would be difficult for me because I am at a level that I have reached financially and emotionally.

Every women last person on the list is herself; yet I do take time for my girlfriends. At least 3-4 there and that is important for me. I feel guilty that it is the one time I am home from traveling. Yet I believe if you cannot be a good friend you cannot have a good friend.

I think people are interesting and I enjoy men and women and their personalities. Company is diverse and attracts a diverse group of people and allows me to interface with a mix of people because that is who are company is.

Violet Interview

Interviewer: Can you give a general outline of how you proceeded with your career and the decisions you made in the process regarding marriage and children?

Violet: I met my husband in high school and married him at age 17 -he was 5 years older than me. He was pursuing music and was producing songs. I grew up in a very middle class environment, my dad died when I was 5. Mom did not know language, men showed up and I thought they were friends of my mom and they were ones feeding the poor. Never thought I would get a college education but be a secretary. Yet, I wanted something different and wanted a career. I was in love with my husband. I was told please of all people - he seems old for me but we did not have children until I was 30 years old. I always wanted to work and knew that I would do something, I did get a job in bank because I was in word processing, we bought studio. I was working at bank for income and insurance.

He started doing jingles; we were young entrepreneurs before I knew what the world ones. He ended up getting busy so I was lonely and decided to go back to school and work full time. Little by little I left bank and did get a job at MEAD. I did get a job and this was my dream if I can only work there. Next thing you know I had a masters degree; secretary did not move into executive positions. I left the division to move to another position. Husband still working, I would continue, I was in training development group and I would have school Thursday – Sunday. I did get organizational development degree in Washington DC. I had been promoted and promoted for 13 years. I was very aggressive about seeking promotions and looked around at people in management and said I can do that; I was naïve; I just assumed I can do it. I could not move up without a Masters; I did not have the office with the same furniture, there was a $40,000 difference and I was doing the same job. I am graduating with my Masters so I will get the promotion yet you need line management experience.. I said here is what I need you to know I am not doing it I am going to bid for new jobs. I felt betrayed and here is the carrot the Masters and I did it and was betrayed.

Then I found out I was pregnant. Dr.M. I wanted to work for (hired at world headquarters) this was the head guy. I did plan my pregnancy. Yet I was on maternity leave and I was breast feeding and I was going to go in and meet this man. I did get pregnant while I was working full time and working on my Masters. I was pregnant and asked for the raise, I want the raise. Pregnant was like every other project, handled it like every other project. I was not feeling valued at the company. Senior guy and I showed up and I decided I want to work for this man. He was from same university. I came back from maternity leave and they promoted me and this man posted a job and I applied for it and I did go after job. I did not have a lot of mentors until this guy. I had advocates not mentors. I did not have someone have someone said these are the land mines. Yet the advocates said if you want it done then give it to Violet. My husband had a career and I had a career, I was proud of it enjoyed my career. Having children makes it very different.

Interviewer: What factors did you consider in making your choices? How have your career choices affected marriage and children?

Violet: I am trying to do it all. I did not want to give up my career. I was very clear about it. My mom was not US citizen and my mom said do not end up like me – fend for yourself. Even when husband was successful I could not stay home it was not my makeup. Children are fun but I was bored with it. This man hired me and he lives in Dallas, he was my mentor – he was a black guy – dynamics there too. He was PhD well respected and brilliant and I loved being in his shadow because I lapped it up. Feedback never hurts me and I did not get enough feedback because I was strong. There is a difference in being strong and bulldozing and I was in the bulldozing stage. I never defined myself as competitive because I did not do sports or music. Yet I am in my own way give me an objective and I will nail it and get it done; I was an overachiever.

What was important for me was to be valued I can do that and it was important. Yet I started working in same job and resented that others in the same job were making more money than me. They were in the industry longer yet I was doing the same job and working same hours and more nailing it and resented the men that made more money. After child I was a mess, I did not want to take my kid into daycare. I had help nanny, keeping the house together. Throwing a child into my life was overwhelming. I was 30 and 35 years old when I had my children. My friends already had kids older. I was old to have children. My good friends were successful women. I did not have a lot of girlfriends unless they were part of a couple. We had time I needed time with my husband with other couples. Then child came and I did not want to do those things, I did not want to be on the road and I did not want to be home.

Interviewer: How has career been an opportunity of loss to marriage and children?

Violet: I was doing a good job at everything. I was not great and that was what bothered me. I want to throw a great party not a good party; I want to be a great wife not a good wife; I want to be a great employee not a good employee, I want to be a great mom not a good mom. I was doing everything good not great. When my life was similar it was fine – it was more complex – it was easier to juggle two balls verses 3 balls or twirling plates the more to juggle more plates is more complex and complicates the situation. I had too many balls in the air. And then because I had been with my husband for so long you look at that relationship and do I still love him and do I want to work on it – come on it is work in a marriage and the longer you are together the more you have to do to keep it exciting. Questions you have and now I have a child. Is this good for me is this good for the relationship, do I want this yet I was being selfish it was not suppose to be about me but about the child. Yet I cannot help but feel that I am not fulfilled with being a mom. I did not turn down anything project at work yet I did things differently. You cannot do it at once.

Balance is when you have all those plates spinning and they do not crash. I remember I would have my luggage under my bed and I was leaving for another trip and my 18 month daughter sat on my luggage and said no go and that was it for me. I took the next 18 months in counseling and I wanted to get a package and I begged for one and did not get it so I had to keep working it took we another 18 months and keep working until I decided I wanted my own consulting practice. I just could not leave the company it was so foreign for me. Then in consulting they gave me project work and I started my own company and then we moved to Dallas. I was traveling too much because I had built up my own company yet I did not have the personnel to help. My husband said we have all the biggest companies around you and they fly people around to do what you do and they are in your background. I never had to network, all these relationships in these great jobs I did the P&L and I had supervisory and management skills. I had this sexy portfolio of clients and here I am at my early 30s and I was not happy. Then I started the charity project – inner process of women that are extremely successful yet they are not happy. Success and happiness means different things for different people. Never thought of never being in the corporate world would miss it. Career enhances me and then it enhances marriage and children. I can now say yes or no to any travel. I look at calendar yet I do miss events because I did not plan so I may miss an event.

Interviewer: You talk about balance, how do you balance to accommodate marriage and children?

Violet: Example of balance; I am out of the loop; last day of school I felt like a creep all my friends bought gifts for the teachers except for me. He did not say anything to me yet I felt I should know that it is my responsibility. I was traveling so what kind of mom am I that I don't know this. I have this stuff with new project ring of the bell at Nastaq etc. my walking partner is a stay at home mother that has a son same age as my son. I help her for ideas and we complement each other. Yet I was guilty and thought what do the teachers think about my son and me and my son is dyslexic. At 9:30pm at night I decided we will give to teachers to buy New Years bags to take this morning. You will stand out and they received a million gifts from students yet you are going to be the only student to give gifts now I felt balanced; three weeks ago I did not feel balanced. It is what you do with being balanced and cockeyed and what do you do and how do you deal with it. I am able to realize when I am out of balanced and we will all be out of balanced all the time in our life yet it is realize it and adjusted to make your life more balanced. My company was developed at home and I was working until 2:30 in the morning scared and broke. I was doing new business and taking away from consulting business and I had to let go to do it. I was the steady income in the corporate world; I was all alone and struggling to work and pay the bills.

Interviewer: What advice would you give to younger women?

Violet: I think the most important thing you need is a great network – your own personal network people that you trust and are not like you and those that will hug you and those that won't hug you and say you think you have problems let's go to the children's floor with those that are dying. There are highs and lows and I do not think we can figure it out by ourselves we need fabulous women to help us. I love my husband and plan to spend my life with him. He is a great husband, business partner and lover yet sometimes I need a great woman friend, listen, I believe you become the 5 people you hang with. You need dream builders not dream drainers in your girlfriends. You need a network of women that will give you support and give to you and you have to give to them. Women experts are different that they are women and they need other women. The biggest seat is when you are in the captain's seat you have the moral obligation to give back and I have a project that is giving back and involves women

www.ingramcontent.com/pod-product-compliance
Lightning Source LLC
Chambersburg PA
CBHW081102290526
45795CB00006B/1970